D1109127

The Colors of Ink

Asia House Gallery: January 10–March 3, 1974

Now *Yin* and *Yang* fashion and form (all things), and the myriad phenomena are strewn and spread (far and wide). The mysterious evolution (of things goes on) without speaking and the divine work (of Nature) operates by itself. For grasses and trees spread forth their glory without depending upon (hues derived from) cinnabar and jasper; clouds and snow whirl and float aloft and are white without waiting for céruse (to make them so). Mountains are turquoise without needing (the colour) "sky blue" and the phoenix is iridescent without the aid of the five colours.... One may be said to have fulfilled one's aim if one can furnish (a painting) with all the five colours by the management of ink (alone)....

Chang Yen-yüan, *Li Tai Ming Hua Chi*, trans. W. R. B. Acker in *Some T'ang and Pre-T'ang Texts on Chinese Painting* (Leiden, 1954), p. 185.

Old Pine Tree. Wen Cheng-ming (1470–1559). Handscroll, ink on paper. H. 10 3/4 in. (27.3 cm.). Detail. *Overleaf*

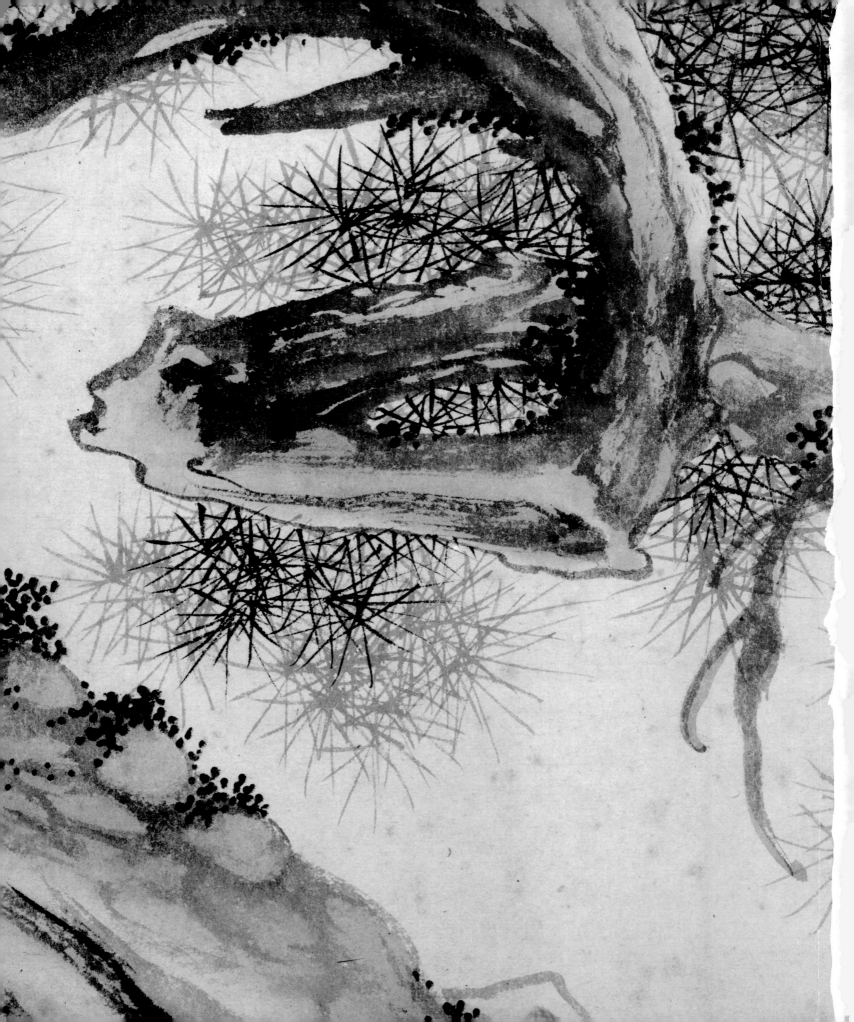

The Colors of Ink

Chinese Paintings and Related Ceramics from The Cleveland Museum of Art

Sherman E. Lee
with catalogue contributions by James Robinson

The Asia Society, Inc.
Distributed by New York Graphic Society Ltd.

The Colors of Ink: Chinese Paintings and Related Ceramics from The Cleveland Museum of Art, is the catalogue of an exhibition shown in the Asia House Gallery in the winter of 1974 as an activity of The Asia Society, to further greater understanding between the United States and the peoples of Asia.

An Asia House Gallery publication

Contents

6	Foreword
7	Preface
9	The Colors of Ink
22	Chronological Table
23	Plates: Paintings
108	Map of China
109	Catalogue: Paintings
119	Plates: Ceramics
131	Catalogue: Ceramics
134	Appendix: Seals and Colophons
136	Bibliography
138	Index

Foreword

In lending New York's Asia House Gallery this selection of forty-seven of its finest Chinese ink paintings, The Cleveland Museum of Art provides the residents of our seaboard cities with a rare opportunity to survey one of man's greatest achievements in the arts. Some connoisseurs declare that the Chinese people have produced the most sophisticated and most profound body of painting that the world has ever known. However, the West is still very little acquainted with it and some of our Western art-lovers may still be surprised at this high estimate of its comparative greatness.

The fact of the matter is that Eastern and Western schools of painting, such as those of China and Japan in contrast to Europe's, have so little similarity that it is questionable whether they should ever be regarded competitively—or subjected to such comparative value judgments. Each side of the world has its own unique glories and each can claim virtues that the other lacks. One finally concludes, perhaps, the only thing they have in common is a paint brush and then must add that even their brushes are very differently designed and differently used.

Through this exhibition, the whole story of China's genius in painting is not told. As with Europe, her painters used color as well as black and white. Dr. Lee has chosen her black-and-white work as more revelatory of her culture, which he explains in his introduction. Probably, he would choose a coloristic exhibition were he sending a show of Western paintings to China—though we, too, have a separate tradition, in our art— that which is encompassed by the word "graphics" where the possibilities of black and white have been richly explored. But our Western tradition of oil and watercolor painting has exploited color as fundamental to form, as in the work of Titian and Matisse, a different approach from that taken by the Chinese.

As we review the history of our exhibitions at the Asia House Gallery of The Asia Society, it is evident that no one has assisted us more copiously with his time and knowledge than Dr. Sherman E. Lee, the Director of the Cleveland Museum. Now, once again, he has kindly and generously assisted us. At very short notice, he has brought together this group of the best Chinese ink paintings in Cleveland's celebrated collection, and has also assembled (with the aid of his equally helpful staff) the pertinent reference material.

How deeply grateful we are to Dr. Lee, it is a privilege to reaffirm. And we are grateful to Mr. Wai-kam Ho, Curator of Chinese Art in the Cleveland Museum, and also to Mr. James Robinson, who dedicated months of his precious time to prepare this remarkable record. It would, indeed, be desirable to list here all those at The Cleveland Museum of Art who have so richly contributed to making this exhibition a reality—including this distinguished institution's dedicated Trustees. But a statement of adequate appreciation is beyond all possibility and we therefore must simply hope that everyone who worked on it and encouraged it will take a proper pride in its presentation.

Gordon Bailey Washburn
Director, Asia House Gallery

Preface

The present display was motivated by an urgent request from the Asia Society for an exhibition to replace a canceled display. The idea had been lying somewhat dormant in my mind for years. The virtues of limitations, the freedom of rules, the breadth of the circumscribed, have always intrigued me. Fortunately the collection in Cleveland had grown to a point where the material was at hand for an exhibition of Chinese ink painting. At first we had thought of an exhibition of Far Eastern ink painting, but the size of such a display, which would have been almost twice that of the present show, made our self-imposed limitations inevitable. The results you see—certainly not comprehensive and most assuredly limited by the time available for preparation, less than three months. The use of Cleveland paintings only was necessitated by considerations of both time and convenience. To work from originals is, one still hopes, better than research from photographs. The addition of the ceramics was perhaps somewhat "quirky" but makes an aesthetic point outside the realm of scientific history. The final result, an incomplete microcosm, is nevertheless something from which one can learn and take pleasure.

This quickly achieved project would never have been possible without the dedicated cooperation and assistance of many individuals. James Robinson, formerly a student of mine at Case Western Reserve University and now a graduate student at the University of Michigan, has been largely responsible for the catalogue entries, based on our departmental records, and for the accompanying map. Wai-kam Ho, Curator of Chinese Art, has acted as mentor to Mr. Robinson, has provided many of the translations as well as the rationale for the remarks on Tung Ch'i-ch'ang, and has advised me on the final draft. Mr. Henry Kleinhenz, a fellow in The Cleveland Museum of Art–Case Western Reserve University Museum Studies Program, also assisted in the final stages of cataloguing. Mrs. Ruth Harris, secretary of the Oriental Department, and Mrs. June Barbish, secretary to the Director, have cheerfully given their assistance in typing and other tasks. Miss Lin-sheng Chang, Assistant to the Director at the National Palace Museum, Taipei, assisted Mr. Robinson in many matters, including the map and the selection of brushstroke photographs. My introduction is an interim essay, short on detail, but I hope it will provide a stimulus for more complete work in the future. We also owe thanks to the staff at the Asia House Gallery, especially to Gordon Washburn and Miss Virginia Field, for their patient and complete cooperation in nursing this exhibition and catalogue to concrete form.

Sherman E. Lee, Director
The Cleveland Museum of Art

此女要嫁只有姻禪師
真問嗲時生青松未
老黄梅颯兩世苦如
夢一場

The Colors of Ink

An act of will is necessary if one is to put down the rich color of landscape in shades of black to white. The blossoming of the color slide industry, whether amateur or professional, is proof enough of the Westerner's desire to experience color when viewing a translation of nature or of a work of art. Mind and will are surely exercised in the firmness with which some archaeologists and art historians, severely intellectual in their requirements, still prefer a black-and-white photograph or slide for understanding the work of art represented. Color is somehow more sensuous, emotional, even transient in the eye of the mind. "Decorative color" is still said in all seriousness; and in Roger de Piles' seventeenth-century rating system for painters, color was but one of four elements to be scored, the others—drawing, composition, and expression—being understandable in monochrome.

The mixed feelings of Western artists and critics about color can be traced in the history of art. With the exception of the rare grisaille works by the fourteenth-century artist Jean de Pucelle and his followers, drawing or painting in black and white was confined to preliminary drawings for a painting or to rapid studies from nature, usually the figure, both to be used in working up the final version in color. By the end of the sixteenth century, landscape drawings existing in their own right were reasonably common, as witness the beautiful and often large-scale drawings by Fra Bartolommeo, Barocci, and Annibale Carracci. Two great masters of ink or sepia landscape drawing in the seventeenth century, Claude and Rembrandt, carried these beginnings to extraordinary fulfillment—perhaps nothing in monochrome since then has been more than variations on themes they invented and brought to fruition. In all the writing about the landscape drawings of these two masters, one reads principally about their tones, touch, composition, space, and, above all, light. Not until the nineteenth century and the flourishing of romanticism do we find indirect, and then direct, mention of the "coloristic" effects of drawing in washes of ink or sepia. However ambiguous the term may be, it is not uncommon to speak of such effects. Nevertheless, one interpretation of the history of Western painting is of its development in the varied use of color, ultimately reaching the integrated color, form, and space of Cézanne. Then the next important development was the reassertion of a sober and rational near-monochrome order by the two inventors of Cubism: Braque and Picasso. Clearly, "black and white" has a place, if a minor one, in the Western tradition.

But as early as 847 one of the greatest of all Chinese historians of painting, Chang Yen-yüan, could say in his *Li Tai Ming Hua Chi*, "one can furnish (a painting) with all the five colours by...ink (alone)," [1] a statement accepted as gospel by the later Chinese painters and writers. As gospel, that is, by the scholar-painters (*wen-jen*: literary men) who traced their lineage to Wang Wei and whose conceptual training in vocabulary, classics, and calligraphy was of the most rigorous and extended nature. Thus, in the seventeenth century, Wu Li wrote in praise of the

Detail of calligraphy from No. 18, *The Second Coming of the Fifth Patriarch*

1. W. R. B. Acker, *Some T'ang and Pre-T'ang Texts on Chinese Painting* (Leiden, 1954), p. 185. The five colors are identified as yellow (jasper), red (cinnabar), blue (azurite), green (malachite), and white (céruse).

9

fourteenth-century painter Wu Chen (No. 12):

Mei Tao-jen's [Wu Chen's] brushwork was pure and strong, original and rich, always full of variation. He expressed new ideas but kept nevertheless within the rules of the style. The wonder of his art reaches beyond the unrestrained; it is perfect, as if accomplished by Heaven. His ink contains all the five colours. *Such was Wu Chen's particular genius. No later painters have been able to reach it.* [2]

One work in the exhibition by Hsiao Yün-ts'ung (No. 38, dated 1668) is a rich ink variation on Wu Chen, a visual statement of the inscription:

I love Mei Tao-jen
Whose brushes often have strange thoughts;
Between the heavy modeling [ts'un] and deep coloring,
One finds himself, as it were, in real forest and wilderness.

(trans. Wen Fong)

Wu Chen himself was fully aware of the implications of his art, for he once quoted Ch'en Yü-i's poem on ink plum blossoms to precise effect: "The thought (or, spirit) is enough, why seek for colored resemblance?" [3] Finally, he ends a poem on landscape painting with a variation on an old Buddhist theme:

One drop of ink contains a world, an infinity of time, all manifest to the heart (as said in Buddhist scriptures). [4]

What called forth this extraordinary Chinese obsession with monochrome ink? What perimeters of art did it require? How could the banishment of "color" enrich the grammar of painting, particularly of landscapes?

One cannot possibly overestimate the importance of calligraphy in the origins of Chinese painting. The written word, or rather idea-character, was of inestimable value to the Chinese. Through writing one could enter the realm of the classics, the world of literature, and from there into the world of the scholar-official, someone who really mattered. Reason combined with knowledge made the ideal man; and calligraphy, together with the more specialized subject of painting, was the means by which this ideal character was expressed. The scholar-painter was never more alive and a part of past, present, and future than when he applied ink to paper or silk with his brush. Since one designed and wrote a character with the care demanded by art and one's own personality, it was natural to think in terms of ink and brush. The written character, derived from the pictogram, was a sign, an idea made into a work of art, whether composed of one or sixty-four strokes. Holding the same brush, using the same ink on the same ground before a real or imaginary landscape, the artist could not approach nature as other than a concept, an abstraction in black and white.

The underlying validity of this attitude can be in part supported by the Western psychological study of dreams—not more than thirty percent of the total are registered in color; most often they are colorless images, intense, but purified (or compressed) by the mind to the essentials of line, shape, space, light, and dark. [5] The combination of the cultural importance of calligraphy with the psychological and intellectual rightness of the colorless image was overwhelming for the history of Chinese painting. If the Greeks conceived of the birth of painting as the lover drawing around the silhouette of the shadow of the Maid of Corinth's head, they soon chose the path of observation. As has been often said, the Chinese paint the land-

2. Osvald Sirén, *Chinese Painting: Leading Masters and Principles*, 7 vols. (London, 1956–58), vol. 5, p. 188. Emphasis added.

3. Osvald Sirén, *The Chinese on the Art of Painting: Translations and Comments* (New York, 1963), p. 111.

4. Ibid., p. 175.

5. The evidence for this, though not conclusive, is at least highly suggestive. See P. H. Knapp, "Sensory Impressions in Dreams," *Psychoanalytic Quarterly*, vol. 25 (1956), pp. 340–43, and C.S. Hall, "What People Dream About," *Scientific American*, vol. 184 (May 1951), p. 62.

scape of the mind. This is not to say that they do not observe and sketch from nature; but when they do they mark the silhouette, the mass, the disposition, with the coloring of nature translated into an infinite variety of ink tones and textures produced by that most flexible of instruments, the Chinese brush, manipulated with disciplined and experienced skill. Thus the *wen-jen* did not consider his production worthy of his peers' approval before he had reached fifty years of age.

First the artist had to understand his materials. Traditional writings give descriptions of the various inks and brushes, but improvements certainly continued for a time, probably until the Sung dynasty (A.D. 960–1279), when Chang Yu (active 1064–1085) mixed the usually scorned oil soot with the traditionally prized pine soot to make an ink cake that produced a deep, glossy ink wash. [6] Pine soot was standard, and that from the inner core of the tree was noted for its depth of tone. Other exotic materials may have enriched the mixture. If we are to believe the stories in old texts, pearl powder, ground jade, and camphor are among the substances said to have been added to the basic soot and gum. True or untrue, the exotic nature of these contents is an indication of the almost magical quality attributed to them. The cakes—often molded into strange shapes, with designs of dragons and other auspicious beings, or with gilded inscriptions—were ground with pure water as the medium upon fine-grained ink stones, just before use. The merits of the various inks from different makers were the topic of endless discussion and nobly prejudiced opinion. The quantity of water used with the ink cake or the stone was obviously of great importance, and the artists and critics have much to say about this, much of it often contradictory, all of it requiring judgment at the extremes of "too wet" and "too dry."

> *If the ink is too dry, it has no* ch'i yün [*spirit-resonance*], *and if one absolutely strives for* ch'i yün, *the result will be an excessive diffuseness. If the ink is too moist, beauty and reason will be lost, but if one absolutely strives for those qualities, the result will be a finicky style (or carved painting:* k'o hua). *The mystery of all the Six Principles cannot be found before one knows how to handle the ink.* [7]
>
> Ku Ning-yüan (Ming period)

The same dichotomy, with its marvelous possibilities and prospects of harrowing failure, was expressed by Tung Ch'i-ch'ang (see No. 32), a great master of both wet and dry ink.

> *Li Ch'eng* [*tenth century*] *spared the ink as if it had been gold; Wang Hsia* [*T'ang period*] *splashed the ink abundantly with water. Students of painting should always keep in their minds these four words:* hsi mo, p'o mo (*spare ink, splash ink*); *if they do it, they will understand more than half of the Six Principles and the Three Classes (of painting).* [8]

Paper and silk, too, were as varied as ink for their particular usages. Absorbent paper from Anhui Province was favored for primarily wet works (No. 41); while the highly sized papers, often Korean, were especially suited to either dry ink or to works where difficult contrasts of dry and wet were attempted (Nos. 32, 47). Paper was usually a pure white, warm or cold, though sometimes a cream or buff tone was desired (No. 39). Silk, also, was very light in color, white or a pale beige: sometimes a satin weave was deemed desirable. Nearly all of the silk has darkened with exposure to light or because of damp storage conditions, and while we may admire the deep sandy or café-au-lait colors, we must remember that the artist would con-

6. The material on ink and brushes is taken largely from Fei Ch'eng-wu, *Brush Drawing in the Chinese Manner* (London and New York, 1956), pp. 55–57.

7. Sirén, *Chinese on the Art of Painting*, p. 162.

8. Ibid., p. 165.

sider them deformities. It may well be that one major consideration for the gradual dominance of paper as a ground for the *wen-jen* paintings was its greater lasting power over silk in this crucial matter of lightness of tone. One should add that control of the dryness or wetness of the ground itself was of considerable importance in determining the final effect. (See No. 47, Li Shih-cho, dry; No. 37, T'ao Hung, wet.) Repeated remountings of older paintings inevitably led to a loss of ink density, and this too is evident in the paintings as we see them now (Nos. 1, 4, 5, 6).

The most important single weapon in the artist's or calligrapher's armory was the brush, and here the Westerner probably finds it difficult to comprehend its complexity and subtlety in the hands of the Chinese. While the handle might be of as humble a material as bamboo, it could also be of more precious substances, from ivory, bronze, jade, cloisonné enamel on copper, to gold. The raison d'être for the brush was its tip, and here the selection of appropriately varied hairs and bristles ranged widely through the animal kingdom. Rabbit, hare, badger, weasel, wolf, deer, horse, goat, pig—even the whiskers of the mouse—supplied tips suitable for the seemingly endless requirements of the calligrapher-artist. Fine-line work (*pai-miao*, Nos. 15, 20) demanded wolf hair or mouse whiskers. Rabbit and goat hair were suitable for rather wet and full ink usage (Nos. 10, 21, 29). Perhaps the hair of the mountain pony with its control of firm, strong strokes was used in the unusual work by Ch'en Hung-shou (No. 36). As one would expect, only in certain regions and certain seasons of the year was it possible to obtain the raw materials in prime condition. The sizes of brushes ranged from tiny, for *pai-miao*, to huge (more than four inches in diameter), for heavy and rough calligraphic work on a large scale. When the brush seemed inadequate for the inspiration of the moment, an improvisation could be made. Thus the rise of finger-nail painting, a specialty of Kao Ch'i-p'ei (1672–1734), or even the reported use of twisted strips of paper, sugarcane husks, or a lotus seed pod by the celebrated early literatus and landscapist Mi Fu (1051–1107). [9]

With these media and tools the artist trained for half a lifetime until he achieved a virtuosity worthy of his hopes and pretensions. While this training may well have become somewhat stereotyped in later dynasties, the implicit end of the discipline was the freedom to write or paint in both rational and intuitive harmony with the divine method of creation. From earliest times, the writings of artists and critics try to cope with verbal descriptions of the bewildering variety of brush strokes created by successive masters as they dealt with the problem of conceptualizing nature and translating the concept into ink. The mere listing of these descriptions may give a hint of the subtlety and variety of the strokes used in various representations. It should be remembered that in earlier times (pre-seventeenth century) the phrases were literary metaphors of peculiar visual appearances; only later did they become formulas to be applied. Even then, only the weakest and most prosaic of painters followed them slavishly. Works by individualists such as Chu Ta (No. 45) or Mei Ch'ing (Nos. 43, 44) recaptured the spirit of the metaphor where academic painters saw only the literal description or the specific woodblock illustration of the given stroke. [10] As in all techniques, the style and spirit of execution were the key to aesthetic success.

Obviously, every excellent painting could not be a mere compendium of classified brush strokes. The union of the whole required the skill, will, and character of a master. As Wang Hui (see No. 46) wrote about the problem of light and dark:

> In painting, the light and the dark form, so to say, the two wings of the bird; one cannot dispense with either of them. If one can give the (right) combination of light and dark; spiritual vitality will ensue. [11]

9. Susan Bush, *The Chinese Literati on Painting* (Cambridge, Mass., 1971), p. 116.

10. See the *Chieh Tzu Yüan Hua Chuan*, or Mustard Seed Garden Manual of Painting, a work of the seventeenth century. It is most easily available in English in Mai-mai Sze, *The Tao of Painting*, 2 vols. (New York, 1956).

11. Sirén, *Chinese on the Art of Painting*, p. 201.

One of the principal means of achieving this spirit-resonance was the sheer joy of perfected movement involved in the making of the brush strokes: a large part of the rhythmic vitality in Chinese brush work is the result of the same "rhythmic vitality" in the accompanying movement of wrist, arm, and even body. Hsieh Ho's famous first canon (of six), *ch'i-yün sheng-tung* (spirit-resonance creates movement) [12] can well be understood as the almost musical resonance of the arm responding to a divine rhythm (or a mind image, if one is a naturalist) and transmitting this movement through the brush to the paper. The oft-quoted remark about the greatest of all Chinese calligraphers, Wang Hsi-chih (303–379), who was known for his love of geese, that "the movement of their turning necks seemed to him to resemble the movement of a man's wrist when he is handling the brush," [13] is instructive and reveals an early awareness of this concept of transmitted movement. It is very like the idea expressed by R. G. Collingwood, among others, in his remarks on body gesture, language, and art. [14]

Then, once all the rules, methods, and techniques are known, the vocabulary, grammar, and style absorbed—as in the West—the rules are broken by those who can risk it. Kuo Hsi (ca. 1020–ca. 1075), one of the great masters of early Chinese monumental landscape painting, stated:

> *Someone may ask: What kind of ink should be used? To which my answer is: Use either burnt ink or ink which has been stored over night, or faded ink, or dust-ink; if one kind is not satisfying, take another.* [15]

And Chao Hsi-ku (ca. 1240) wrote:

> *In calligraphy, concealing the brush tip consists of wielding the brush in a steadfast and thoroughly satisfying way. If one can understand a good calligrapher's method of wielding the brush, then one can understand the view that great paintings are without brush traces.* [16]

The tool and technique must be hidden for the idea to be manifest. One recalls the description of Velasquez's art at its best—that the paint seemed to have been breathed onto the canvas. The legendary end of Wu Tao-tzu, the greatest of China's figure painters, who disappeared into one of his own wall paintings, is a myth that reveals the nature of art's highest achievement.

While ink was the dominant means of expression in calligraphy from the Han dynasty and earlier, until the T'ang dynasty its part in painting was largely subsidiary. It was used for sketches, preliminary outlining, Buddhist iconographic studies, and, of course, for the "bones" of colored paintings—drapery and figure outlines, tree and mountain silhouettes, and for all those purposes where boundaries were necessary for the separation of color. The dominance of color in Chinese painting at this time was certainly reinforced by the effect of Buddhist art from India and Central Asia. The combined influences of Indian use of color and modeling and of the sensuous descriptions of color in the paradises, as set forth in the holy texts, is unmistakably strong in the earliest preserved paintings, whether wall paintings from Tun Huang, Wan-Fo-Hsia, and Mai-Ch'i-Shan or the rare portable paintings still extant, notably those from Tun Huang. It is significant that Wu Tao-tzu is said to have painted only the *ink* parts (outlines and so on) of the large-scale wall paintings that made him renowned as the greatest of all Chinese figure painters. Color was added by artisan assistants and was not an important element in judging the final result. [17] While color was slightly less important in the official paintings produced

12. See A.C. Soper, "The First Two Laws of Hsieh Ho," *Far Eastern Quarterly*, vol. 8, no. 4 (August 1949), pp. 412–23, and Acker, *Some T'ang and Pre-T'ang Texts*, pp. xxi–xliii, for thorough analyses of the meaning of this and Hsieh Ho's other five canons. The meaning suggested by the translation here and briefly discussed further on is that developed by Wai-kam Ho in "Tung Ch'i-ch'ang's New Orthodoxy and the Southern School Theory," Princeton Symposium, 1971 (in press). I am deeply indebted to my colleague's patient and lucid explanation of what, to me, seems the most valid translation and interpretation of *ch'i-yün sheng-tung*.

13. Sirén, *Chinese on the Art of Painting*, p. 50.

14. R.G. Collingwood, *The Principles of Art* (New York, 1958), pp. 246–47.

15. Sirén, *Chinese on the Art of Painting*, p. 50.

16. Bush, *Chinese Literati on Painting*, p. 115.

17. See Kuo Jo-hsü, *T'u-hua chien-wen chih*, trans. A.C. Soper (Washington, D.C., 1951), pp. 17, 18, and the citation from Chang Yen-yüan in Sirén, *Chinese Painting*, vol. 1, p. 118.

(*text continued on p. 16*)

Details of Brush Strokes

1. Chü-jan. Alum-lump *ts'un*.

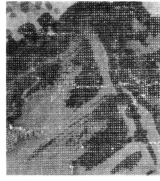

3. Ma Lin. Small and large ax-cut *ts'un*.

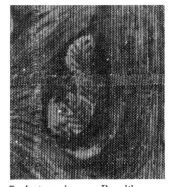

7. Artist unknown. Ropelike cypress (or cedar) bark.

10. Chao Meng-fu. Flying white.

12. Wu Chen. Hemp-fiber *ts'un*.

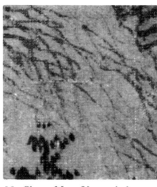

13. Sheng Mou. Unraveled-rope *ts'un*.

14. Yen Hui. Nail-head rat-tail stroke.

15. Chang Wu. Spring-silkworm-spitting-silk stroke.

16. P'u Ming. Ghost-face *ts'un*.

23. Artist unknown. Crab-claw branch.

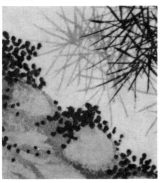

28. Wen Cheng-ming. Black-pepper dots.

32. Tung Ch'i-ch'ang. "One" character dots.

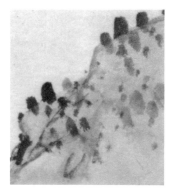

34. Lan Ying. Rain-snow dots.

37. T'ao Hung. Fish-scale pine bark.

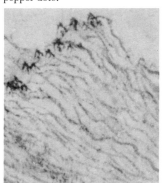

46. Wang Hui. Nail-extracted-from-mud *ts'un*.

47. Li Shih-cho. Flame branch.

The following list is taken from Cheng Ch'ang's *A History of Chinese Painting* (Shanghai, 1929). The numbers in parentheses refer to the entries in Benjamin March, *Some Technical Terms of Chinese Painting* (Baltimore, 1935). Examples of these strokes are found in the paintings included in this exhibition and are reproduced on the facing page. Their catalogue numbers have been inserted into the list below.

I. Strokes for Figures
1. Angle-worm stroke (259) *ch'iu-yin miao*
2. Lute-string stroke (260) *ch'in-hsien miao*
3. Mr. Ts'ao's clothes stroke (from Ts'ao Pu-hsing) (261) *Ts'ao i miao*
4. Spring-silkworm-spitting-silk stroke (262) *ch'ün-ts'an t'u-ssu fa*
    (Cat. No. 15. Chang Wu.)
5. Drifting-cloud and flowing-water stroke (263) *hsing-yün liu-shui miao*
6. Willow-leaf stroke (264) *liu-yeh miao*
7. Bamboo-leaf stroke (265) *chu-yeh miao*
8. Shaky-brush water-wave stroke (266) *chan-pi shui-wen miao*
9. Wasp's-body stroke (267) *ma-huang miao*
10. Date-pit stroke (268) *tsao-ho miao*
11. Olive (pit) stroke (269) *kan-lan miao*
12. Iron-wire stroke (270) *t'ieh-hsien miao*
13. Bent (or broken) reed stroke (271) *che-lu miao*
14. Nail-head rat-tail stroke (272) *ting-tou shu-wei miao*
    (Cat. No. 14. Yen Hui.)
15. Driven-stake stroke (273) *chüeh-t'ou-ting miao*
16. Simplified brush stroke (274) *chien-pi miao*
17. Brushwood (or kindling) stroke (275) *k'u ch'ai miao*
18. Mixed (or double-line) stroke (276) *hun miao*

II. Ts'un or Texture Wrinkles
1. Hemp-fiber *ts'un* (209, 210) *ma-p'i* (or *p'i-ma*) *ts'un*
    (Cat. No. 12. Wu Chen.)
2. Lotus-leaf (veins) *ts'un* (215) *ho-yeh ts'un*
3. Unraveled-rope *ts'un* (216) *chieh-suo ts'un*
    (Cat. No. 13. Sheng Mou.)
4. Confused-cloud *ts'un* (217) *lüan-yün ts'un*
5. Thunder-head *ts'un* (217) *yün-t'ou ts'un*
6. Rolling-cloud *ts'un* (218) *chüan-yün ts'un*
7. Cattle-hair *ts'un* (219) *niu-mao ts'un*
8. Torn-net *ts'un* (220) *p'o-wang ts'un*
9. Alum-lump *ts'un* (221) *fan-t'ou ts'un*
    (Cat. No. 1. Chü-jan.)
10. Pellet (as dropped into mud)-whirlpool (eddies) *ts'un* (222) *tan-wo ts'un*
11. Ghost-face *ts'un* (223) *kuei-mien ts'un*
    (Cat. No. 16. P'u Ming.)
12. Split-bean *ts'un* (224) *tou-pan ts'un*
13. Raindrop *ts'un* (225) *yü-tien ts'un*
14. Peach-thorn *ts'un* (226) *tz'u-li ts'un*
15. Small and large ax-cut *ts'un* (227, 228) *hsiao* and *ta fu-p'i ts'un*
    (Cat. No. 3. Ma Lin.)
16. Dragged-through-mud-and-water *ts'un* (231) *t'o-ni tai-shui ts'un*
17. Nail-extracted-from-mud *ts'un* (232) *ni-li pa-ting ts'un*
    (Cat. No. 46. Wang Hui.)
18. Horse-tooth *ts'un* (233) *ma-ya ts'un*
19. Iron-wire *ts'un* (234) *t'ieh-hsien ts'un*
20. Rain-soaked wall-top *ts'un*: *yü-lin ch'iang-t'ou ts'un*
21. Skeleton: *ts'un ku-lua ts'un*

III. Trees and Rock Types
1. Fish-scale pine bark (171) *sung-p'i ju lin ts'un*
    (Cat. No. 37. T'ao Hung.)
2. Ropelike cypress (or cedar) bark (172) *po-p'i ju sheng ts'un*
    (Cat. No. 7. Artist unknown.)
3. Flying white: *fei-pai*
    (Cat. No. 10. Chao Meng-fu.)
4. Mother-of-pearl: *yün-mu*
5. "Mountain" character: *shan tzu*
6. Clove branch (167) *ting-hsiang chih*
7. Sparrow-claw branch (168) *ch'iao-chua chih*
8. Crab-claw branch
    (Cat. No. 23. Artist unknown.)
9. Flame branch (169) *huo-yen chih*
    (Cat. No. 47. Li Shih-cho.)
10. Dragged branch (170) *t'o chih*

IV. Tien or Dots
1. Large confused dots (176) *ta-hun tien*
2. Small confused dots (177) *hsiao-hun tien*
3. Cedar-leaf dots (178) *po-yeh tien*
4. Level-headed dots (179) *p'ing-tou tien*
5. Raised-headed dots (180) *yang-t'ou tien*
6. Bowed-headed dots (181) *ch'ui-t'ou tien*
7. Rat-foot dots (191) *shu-tsu tien*
8. Rain-snow dots (236) *yü-hsüeh tien*
    (Cat. No. 34. Lan Ying.)
9. Broken-brush dots (237) *p'o-pi tien*
10. Black-pepper dots (238) *hu-chiao tien*
    (Cat. No. 28. Wen Cheng-ming.)
11. "One" character dots (239) *i-tzu tien*
    (Cat. No. 32. Tung Ch'i-ch'ang.)
12. Hanging-creeper dots (241) *ch'ui-t'eng tien*
13. Dragon-horn stroke
14. Phoenix-tail stroke
15. Golden-jade-knife stroke

at the court, such as the Emperor scroll at Boston or the court ladies shown in the scrolls of Chou Fang style in Kansas City, Boston, Taipei, and Peking, it still occupied a position equal to the ink bones of these scrolls. The "invention" of monochrome ink painting for the production of "finished" landscape pictures is variously attributed to Wang Wei (699–759) or Wang Hsia (ninth century). [18]

The reliability of these statements is uncertain, particularly because ink painting was inseparably tied to the *wen-jen* tradition and the sacred genealogy of style was preserved at all costs. Still, the grain of truth is there, for accompanying it is the inescapable fact that by the tenth century ink landscapes, largely monochrome, were painted in an accomplished and monumental style (No. 1 is a tenth- or early eleventh-century work in the style associated with Chü-jan). The beautiful and decorative "blue, green, and gold" landscapes of the T'ang dynasty, often backgrounds for historical narrative or expressions of courtly antiquity, were superseded by the new style. In the Ming and Ch'ing dynasties, when the *wen-jen* tradition was triumphant, color wash was sometimes used, but the solid colors of the old courtly T'ang style were to be found largely in the paintings produced by the artists attached to the court ("Academicians") or by artisans who made paintings for decorative purposes. The usual Occidental predeliction for color is never more evident than in the continued popularity of such minor Chinese works in many Western countries.

By the late tenth century, whether under the impetus of Wang Wei or Wang K'ai a century earlier, or by a consensus unknown to us, landscapes in monochrome ink were being made in a thoroughly accomplished and sophisticated manner by artists of both North and South China such as Fan K'uan, Li Ch'eng, Tung Yüan, and Chü-jan. Few originals remain; however, works close to them are extant, largely in Taiwan and on the mainland with a few stragglers in the West. *Buddhist Retreat by Stream and Mountains* (No. 1) is one of these. It would be folly here to draw any general conclusions from this solitary representative of the early monumental and complex style of landscape painting. But when compared with a characteristic and poetic work of the Southern Sung dynasty by Ma Lin, two centuries later (No. 3), at least one observation can be made that seems to apply to the general evolution of ink painting over this extended period. Where the Chü-jan style is complex, with numerous brush strokes seeming to coalesce into an overall view of nature both felt and rationalized, the Ma Lin is simpler, its fewer brush strokes counting for more individually than as parts of an overwhelming whole. Further, they imply far more than they actually describe. The Ma Lin suggests a more abstract vision of nature, a style that developed gradually from the more rational and naturalistic earlier works. In this process the *brush stroke* becomes more isolated, and the artist's attention is therefore brought increasingly to bear upon the nature of that single stroke. The general process is akin to that of Herbert Spencer's theory of differentiation: one proceeds from the general and universal to the particular and the specialized.

Ch'an (in Japanese, Zen) Buddhist painting of the late Southern Sung period contained this stroke specialization within the more limited requirements of figure painting (No. 6) and provided paradigms for the next century of Ch'an painting (Nos. 5, 18, 24). At the same time Ch'an painters could multiply the liberated single strokes into a veritable "sea of ink" to produce such moist and ambiguous images as those to be seen in the tiger and dragon paintings associated with the name Mu Ch'i (Fa-ch'ang; Nos. 4, 5). But a comparison of these complex images with the equally complicated landscape of Chü-jan (No. 1) reveals the overall change that has taken place from sharpness, logical placement, and spatial development to intentional suggestiveness and ambiguity, from controlled and semidry ink to moist serendipity. Ink painting during the three-hundred-year period of the Sung dynasty

18. See Sirén, *Chinese on the Art of Painting*, p. 146, quoting Tung Ch'i-ch'ang, and p. 175, quoting Shen Hao.

developed a wide vocabulary of brush strokes and a broad grammar of pictorial structure. The virtuoso usage of these basic elements for a new purpose was achieved in the succeeding Yüan dynasty.

While numerous gifted artists of the late thirteenth and fourteenth centuries developed variations on this earlier syntax (Nos. 11, 13, 15, 18, 20, 22, 24), a smaller number of literati, members of the scholarly elite, experimented with the structure provided by the great Northern Sung masters as a means, not of pictorial creation, but of written confession—using landscape, almost alone, as the means of personal expression through brush work. The new and revolutionary literati approach to the use of ink for the *writing* of pictures was the creation of the now famous *wen-jen* artists of the Yüan dynasty—Chao Meng-fu (No. 10), Wu Chen (Nó. 12), Ni Tsan, Wang Meng, Huang Kung-wang, and others. When judged by the standards of Sung, their work appears disassociated, willful, even perverse. Brush writing overthrows the visual image; ink relationships on the paper take precedence over tonal precisions in nature; and yet, the pervasive "flavor" (the Indian *rasa*) of the finished work is present and as palpable as that of the best of earlier paintings. But now the flavor is wholly that of the individual scholar—his character, his repertory. This flavor, though strong, is not easily definable and indeed is often cloaked and made deliberately obscure. The situation is not unlike that to be found in the early cubist works of Braque and Picasso, where the identity of means and ends within a deliberately limited pictorial language leaves only the personal intonation as a clue to the individual origin of the work. If one is a member of the club, or at least an aficionado of the game, the personal nuance is immediately recognizable and, more, enjoyable and revealing. But it is a closely circumscribed game with firm if unwritten rules.

One of the rules concerns ink. The personal variations within this are as numerous as the individuals, and more marked if the artist is distinguished. Wu Chen's wet but dark ink (No. 12), the strokes clearly separated and the ink sharp to the edges of the stroke, is clearly recognizable. Chao Meng-fu's wide variety of stroke and wash (No. 10), particularly the "flying white" broken ink wash in the suggestion of crumbly rock textures, is equally distinctive. Both famous artists found their emulators, whether contemporary ones such as P'u Ming (No. 16) and Liu Shan-shou (No. 21) who followed Chao, or later literati such as Shen Chou (Nos. 26, 27) who followed, at least in part, the sharp staccato manner of Wu Chen.

Another of the unwritten rules was a particular homage to the past in the form of acknowledged variations and improvisations upon the styles of earlier masters who were recognized as ancestors or as part of the direct line of *wen-jen* descent. Works with carefully acknowledged indebtedness to tenth-century landscapists such as Tung Yüan or Chü-jan are part of the stock in trade of Wu Chen and Chao Meng-fu. This "footnoting" became even more prevalent in the Ming and Ch'ing periods, as even a casual study of some paintings from that time will show (Nos. 31, 32, 34, 39, 40-43, 46). To a large extent artists saw the natural landscape as reflecting the styles of famous early masters—in much the same way that we might say a view in Aix is like Cézanne, or one in the Campagna like Claude.

Yet another element, based in the past but heightened and made explicit, was that of direct and varied literary connections for seemingly repetitive landscape representations. As the picture was "written," so was it usually accompanied by literary texts—poems either from the past or composed by the artist—related to the subject of the scroll. Perhaps even more important, there was always a specific title, often of four characters, designating the work and becoming a major part of its identity. It is hard for the Westerner to realize that a given work can be specifically identified only by a title with an apparently innocuous content—*Old Trees by a Cool*

Spring (No. 11), *Poetic Feeling in a Thatched Pavilion* (No. 12), *Thin Forest and Distant Mountains* (No. 33)—but a content that relates as much or more to the flavor and method of the painting as do the very specific classical titles of landscapes by Claude and Poussin. *Wen-jen-hua*, literary man's painting, means very literally what it says. Still, when all this is acknowledged and digested, we are left with amazingly varied and individual works, joys to the eye, stimulating to the mind—and achieved within deliberately restricted but confidently applied rules of the game.

While the major change in Chinese painting occurred in the fourteenth century, a very few strange works, such as *The Lantern Night Excursion of Chung K'uei* by Yen Hui (No. 14), stand alone, partaking little of either the new and progressive *wen-jen* philosophy or of the older, conservative substream represented by works such as those by Li Shih-hsing (No. 11), Chang Wu (No. 15), or Lo Chih-ch'uan (No. 22). The Yen Hui handscroll represents a style based on a combination of modeling in light and shade, ultimately derived from Indian and Mediterranean pictorial imports, with the "tattered" calligraphic brush line of late Sung Ch'an and other paintings such as Nos. 4, 5, 6, and 9. Dying without successors, Yen's method remains a "sport," but of the highest interest, partly because of its rarity.

The continuum of Chinese painting from the fourteenth century onward was not really broken until late Ming times, more precisely in the early seventeenth century, under the particular influence of the great critic-calligrapher-artist Tung Ch'i-ch'ang (see No. 32). While many major artists' works are known from the early and middle Ming period—Shen Chou (Nos. 26, 27) and Wen Cheng-ming (No. 28), for example—it was Tung and his followers who postulated a continuous tradition of *wen-jen* painting, and who commented on both the aesthetic and art historical problems involved in this tradition. [19]

The painters of early and middle Ming, whether of the Che school [20] (nominally following the traditions of the court painters of later Sung) or of the Wu school (centered around Shen Chou and Wen Cheng-ming and the continuing of the Yüan *wen-jen* tradition), were apparently not conscious of any sharp division among themselves as to their legitimacy or their place in the historical continuum that proceeded from T'ang through Sung and Yüan to their own dynasty. Their writings are usually devoid of rigid theorizing or strictures involving a "true" *wen-jen* tradition. However, it is significant that the teacher of Shen Chou, Tu Chiung, had proposed two conflicting traditions—one of gold-and-blue decorative painting derived from the Li school of the T'ang dynasty, and an ink monochrome school derived from Wang Wei of middle T'ang. [21]

The paintings of these fifteenth- and sixteenth-century masters display a degree of cross-fertilization from Wu to Che and back again that bears out the continuity we have been discussing briefly here. Even a single work such as *Old Pine Tree* by Wen Cheng-ming (No. 28), with its varied brush technique and ink washes, its dramatically "cut-off" compositions, and its attention to naturalism in texture and delineation, can be seen as part of an organic whole that encompasses such varied elements of the past as Southern Sung composition, Northern Sung delineation of tree forms, Yüan emphasis on ink textures, and the bold and brusque brush manner of Wen's master, Shen Chou, who in turn looked back to Wu Chen of Yüan (No. 12).

If we look at a classic painting by Tung Ch'i-ch'ang (No. 32), or art works by later artists such as Ch'en Hung-shou (No. 36), Kung Hsien (Nos. 39, 40), or Mei Ch'ing (Nos. 43, 44), we are aware of a more arbitrary, conscious approach—more willful, even arrogant at times. Tung's *Mountains on a Clear Autumn Day*, seen as a composition or as a rendering of nature, in comparison to his immediate predecessors is an arbitrary and willful performance. Sensuous graciousness remains only

Fig. 1. A Pair of Peacocks. Lin Liang (act. 1488–1505). Ink on silk. H. 60 5/8 in. (153.9 cm.), W. 42 1/8 in. (107 cm.). Mr. and Mrs. Severance A. Millikin Collection

19. To follow this development, Wai-kam Ho's "Tung Ch'i-ch'ang's New Orthodoxy" is indispensable.

20. See the painting by Lin Liang (fig. 1), not included in the exhibition.

21. See Wai-kam Ho, "Tung Ch'i-ch'ang's New Orthodoxy." One of the few paintings by Tu Chiung, but with color washes, is a landscape handscroll in The Cleveland Museum of Art, acc. no. 68.195.

in the ink itself, as Wang Yüan-ch'i (1642–1715) knew very well when he said,

> *It is possible to learn the brushwork of Tung Ch'i-ch'ang, but his ink is so fresh and*
> *variegated, so pure, bright and attractive that it moves people irresistibly; how*
> *could such a thing be produced by human power?* [22]

Except for this "attractiveness" of ink, the painting is not immediately accessible; it conforms to the *wen-jen* ideal of an elitist art, accessible only to members of the in-group. Like Tung's historic division of the history of painting into the Northern and Southern schools, the latter being the sanctified tradition, and his philosophical justification of the Ch'an "sudden enlightenment" approach to painting, his painting reveals intellectual power expressed through a mastery of ink; very few of his works use color, and those that do are daring and arbitrary in the unaccustomed method. Perhaps the best explanation of his art is given by Tung Ch'i-ch'ang himself:

> *... painting is no equal to mountains and water for the wonder of scenery; but*
> *mountains and water are no equal to painting for the sheer marvels of brush and ink.*
> (trans. Wai-kam Ho)

While the importance of the past in providing models was recognized, there were at least two other considerations: the models were selected only from the true *wen-jen* tradition—Wang Wei, Tung Yüan, Chü-jan, Mi Fu, and the Four Great Masters of Yüan (see Nos. 31, 38, 40, 41, 42, 46); and the stamp of the individual, his thoughts, his brush, and his feelings were to dominate all else. To a considerable extent, then, if the history of painting before Tung Ch'i-ch'ang was made into a purposeful orthodoxy selected from objective history, the history of painting after his formulation became a series of personal conversations among literati. Thus one can speak of a historical development of painting before 1600; after that, one is aware of an almost random arrangement of individuals working within the new orthodoxy, or "outsiders" working with those remnants of the past disdained by the orthodox. The history of later Chinese painting is found in the works produced by the new orthodoxy—whether conservative, as in the careful and complex oeuvre of Wang Hui (No. 46), or individualist, as in the paintings by Kung Hsien (Nos. 39, 40), Ch'a Shih-piao (Nos. 41, 42), Mei Ch'ing (Nos. 43, 44), or Chu Ta (No. 45).

With a few exceptions, such as court painters and decorators, the "outsiders" are not seen as part of the standard history of Chinese painting. This situation is comparable to the one surrounding the study of nineteenth-century French painting until very recently. Art historians designated the "official" line of descent—Courbet, Manet, Impressionism, and Post-Impressionism—as *the* history of French painting. What must be understood is that both of these "histories" represent value judgments, defensible, perhaps admirable, but they leave large areas of artistic activity in limbo.

To take but one example, the appearance of both ink tones and space in the work of Kung Hsien (Nos. 39, 40) strikes some critics as somehow different from any previous work in Chinese painting. The level, flat, and receding distance of the little marsh scene, though related to the "level distance" of Northern Sung artists such as Li Ch'eng and Kuo Hsi, seems achieved with simpler means. The ink tones of the towering landscape "after Tung Yüan and Chü-jan," though certainly bowing to those early ancestors of *wen-jen-hua,* seem to convey effects, not of color, but of *light,* as seen in Western black-and-white drawings.

Strong questions about Western influence before the eighteenth century have been posed only recently, notably by Yonezawa, Cahill, and Sullivan. [23] It is not without significance that these questions, above all others, have met with the strong-

22. Sirén, *Chinese on the Art of Painting,* p. 214.

23. See *Proceedings of the International Symposium on Chinese Painting,* National Palace Museum (Taipei, 1972), pp. 595–625, 637–98. Footnote 15, p. 680, refers to Yonezawa's contributions in *Kokka* nos. 732 (1953) and 831 (1961). A reading of the discussion sections in the symposium reports gives only a faint idea of the depth of the resistance to the suggestions of Cahill and Sullivan.

est resistance from the orthodox and traditional scholars of Chinese painting. There is still much to be done before a reasonably complete picture of the history of later Chinese painting can be presented. In the meantime we can find considerable satisfaction in Tung Ch'i-ch'ang's justification of the purposes of literary man's painting, seen in terms of the life of one of its great heroes, Huang Kung-wang (1269–1354): "to take refuge in painting, and to take pleasure in painting." [24]

While the text of this exhibition consists of Chinese ink painting, punctuation has been provided in the form of some notable Chinese ceramics in black and white. The variations of white from cool to warm are visible in the Ch'ing-pai wares of the Sung and Yüan dynasties (Nos. 49, 64) and the Ting wares of Sung and Chin (Nos. 56–60). These tonal variations provided the standard for almost all porcelains of later times, whether in monochrome, as a ground for decoration beneath the glaze, or in enamels upon it.

More interesting and paradoxical are the slip-decorated wares identified by the term "Tz'u-chou" (Nos. 50–55, 62, 63), after the area in Honan Province where stonewares have been made for over a thousand years—interesting, because they display an amazing flexibility and complexity in the basic decorative scheme of black and white; paradoxical, because they are not "classic" wares, revered within the *wen-jen* tradition, but are usually of humbler origin and purpose. Even though Tz'u-chou-type wares of the finest quality were produced for wealthy persons, such wares generally were more popular with upper-middle-class merchants and farmers than they were with the aristocracy or the scholar-officials. [25] The often exuberant decoration, splendid and rich, would seem to be appropriate for this milieu.

We know now that the slip-decorated wares, originated and produced primarily in the Honan-Hopei-Shanhsi area, are also found further south in Anhui, Chianghsi, and Kuangtung. [26] Despite this relatively broad geographic spread, the finest wares are associated with their Honan-Hopei origins, and those shown here seem to be from this area.

Just as the elite *wen-jen* used his ink in myriad ways with seemingly infinite variations of tone and "color," so did the decorators vary the basically simple elements at their disposal—white slip and brown-to-black slip; brush, knife, and point. Beginning with the plain white slip covered by a transparent glaze, as seen in the T'ang dynasty jar (No. 48), the progression, not necessarily chronological but surely typological, is: from painted dark slip on white slip; light slip on dark slip; white slip carved away to dark body; dark slip carved away to lighter body; areas reserved by stencil or carving and then inlaid with light or dark slip; linear designs incised through white slip; linear designs incised through dark slip; carved thin slip; carved thick slip; incised linear designs inlaid with white slip by wiping; and finally to any combination or variation of the methods just enumerated. The spectacular results seem a fitting counterpoint to the ink paintings. It would be an error, however, to equate the noble-appearing vase (No. 51) with the nobly originated album painting (No. 3) by Ma Lin, painter to the Emperor, in anything but the broadest sense of artistic problem-solving. These two experiments in different media are differently motivated from a social and technological point of view. But their juxtaposition is at least a step toward establishing a sense of aesthetic community within the limits of black and white; and on this level we can be permitted to echo the words of Wu Chen (see No. 12) on the power of black and white:

> *I took ink to be a plaything,*
> *And unexpectedly became a slave through ink.* [27]

24. Wai-kam Ho, "Tung Ch'i-ch'ang's New Orthodoxy," p. 23.

25. See Feng Hsien-ming, "T'ang and Sung Kiln-sites in Mi-hsien and Teng-jeng hsien, Honan," *Wen Wu*, no. 3, 1964, pp. 47-55, trans. H.C. Lovell in *Chinese Translations* No. 5, Oriental Ceramic Society (London, 1970), p. 18.

26. Feng Hsien-ming, "Important Finds of Ancient Chinese Ceramics Since 1949," *Wen Wu*, no. 9, 1965, pp. 25-56, trans. H.C. Lovell in *Chinese Translations* No. 1, Oriental Ceramic Society (London, n.d.), p. 40.

27. Bush, *Chinese Literati on Painting*, p. 133.

Chronological Table
of Painters and Dated Paintings

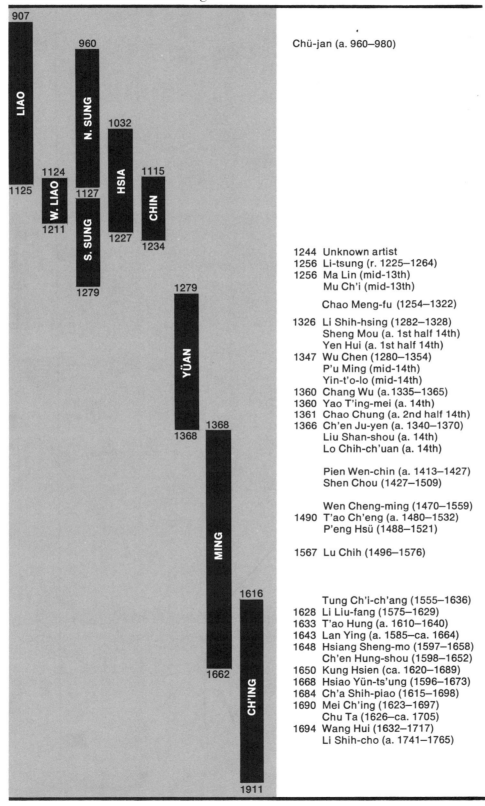

Chü-jan (a. 960–980)

1244 Unknown artist
1256 Li-tsung (r. 1225–1264)
1256 Ma Lin (mid-13th)
     Mu Ch'i (mid-13th)

     Chao Meng-fu (1254–1322)

1326 Li Shih-hsing (1282–1328)
     Sheng Mou (a. 1st half 14th)
     Yen Hui (a. 1st half 14th)
1347 Wu Chen (1280–1354)
     P'u Ming (mid-14th)
     Yin-t'o-lo (mid-14th)
1360 Chang Wu (a. 1335–1365)
1360 Yao T'ing-mei (a. 14th)
1361 Chao Chung (a. 2nd half 14th)
1366 Ch'en Ju-yen (a. 1340–1370)
     Liu Shan-shou (a. 14th)
     Lo Chih-ch'uan (a. 14th)

     Pien Wen-chin (a. 1413–1427)
     Shen Chou (1427–1509)

     Wen Cheng-ming (1470–1559)
1490 T'ao Ch'eng (a. 1480–1532)
     P'eng Hsü (1488–1521)

1567 Lu Chih (1496–1576)

     Tung Ch'i-ch'ang (1555–1636)
1628 Li Liu-fang (1575–1629)
1633 T'ao Hung (a. 1610–1640)
1643 Lan Ying (a. 1585–ca. 1664)
1648 Hsiang Sheng-mo (1597–1658)
     Ch'en Hung-shou (1598–1652)
1650 Kung Hsien (ca. 1620–1689)
1668 Hsiao Yün-ts'ung (1596–1673)
1684 Ch'a Shih-piao (1615–1698)
1690 Mei Ch'ing (1623–1697)
     Chu Ta (1626–ca. 1705)
1694 Wang Hui (1632–1717)
     Li Shih-cho (a. 1741–1765)

Plates: Paintings

1. Buddhist Retreat by Stream and Mountains. Attributed to Chü-jan (act. ca. 960–980). Hanging scroll, ink on silk. H. 73 in. (185.4 cm.). Detail opposite

2. Poem by Wang Wei, 1256. Emperor Li-tsung (r. 1225–1264). Album leaf, ink on silk. H. 9 7/8 in. (25.1 cm.)

行到水窮處

坐看雲起時

3. Scholar Reclining and Watching Rising Clouds, 1256. Ma Lin (act. mid-13th century). Album leaf, ink and slight color on silk. H. 9 7/8 in. (25.1 cm.)

4. Dragon. Attributed to Mu Ch'i (act. mid-13th century). Hanging scroll, ink on silk. H. 48 3/4 in. (123.8 cm.). Detail opposite

5. Tiger. Attributed to Mu Ch'i (act. mid-13th century). Hanging scroll, ink and slight color on silk. H. 48 3/4 in. (123.8 cm.). Detail opposite

6. Shakyamuni Coming Down from the Mountains, 1244. Artist unknown. Hanging scroll, ink on paper. H. 29 3/8 in. (74.6 cm.). Detail opposite

7. Returning Birds and Old Cypress.
Artist unknown. Album leaf, ink on silk.
H. 9 3/8 in. (23.8 cm.). Detail opposite

8. Waterfall. Artist unknown. Hanging scroll, ink on silk. H. 33 in. (83.8 cm.). Detail opposite

9. Bodhidharma Meditating Facing a Cliff. Artist unknown. Hanging scroll, ink on silk. H. 45 3/4 in. (116.2 cm.). Detail opposite

10. Bamboos, Rocks, and Lonely Orchids. Chao Meng-fu (1254–1322). Handscroll, ink on paper. H. 19 7/8 in. (50.5 cm.). Detail opposite

11. Old Trees by a Cool Spring, 1326.
Li Shih-hsing (1282–1328). Hanging scroll,
ink on silk. H. 65 1/4 in. (165.7 cm.).
Detail opposite

泰定丙寅冬十二月蘭丘李生行遵道作

**12. Poetic Feeling in a Thatched Pavil-
ion,** 1347. Wu Chen (1280–1354). Handscroll,
ink on paper. H. 9 3/8 in. (23.8 cm.)

13. Travelers in Autumn Mountains.
Sheng Mou (act. first half of 14th century).
Album leaf, ink on silk. H. 9 5/8 in.
(24.4 cm.)

16. Bamboo in the Wind. P'u Ming (act. mid-14th century). Hanging scroll, ink on silk. H. 30 in. (76.2 cm.)

**14. The Lantern Night Excursion of
Chung K'uei.** Yen Hui (act. first half of 14th
century). Handscroll, ink on silk. H. 9 3/4
in. (24.8 cm.). Continued overleaf

**14. The Lantern Night Excursion of
Chung K'uei.** First section of handscroll.
Detail of last section, opposite

15. The Nine Songs, 1360. Chang Wu
(act. 1335–1365). Handscroll, ink on paper.
H. 11 in. (27.9 cm.). Parts 1 and 2.
Parts 3 and 4, opposite

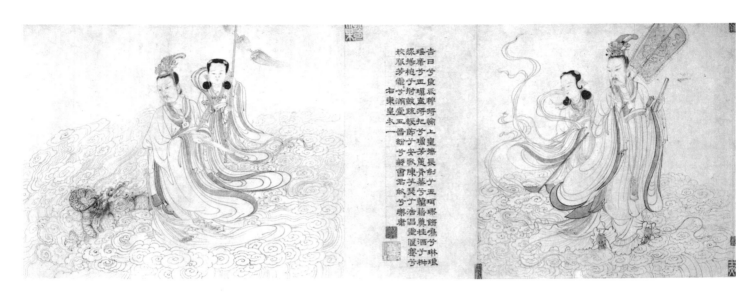

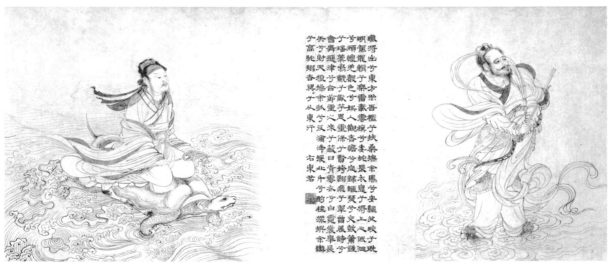

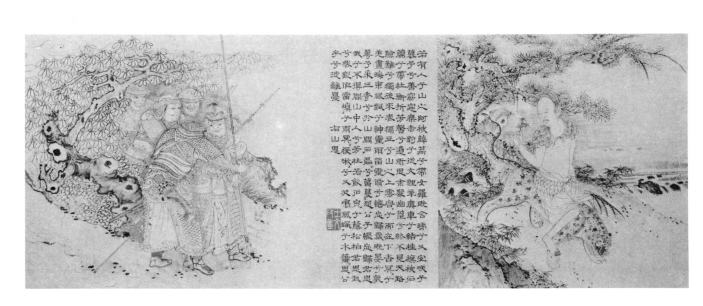

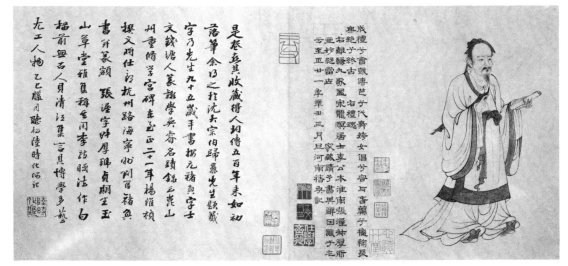

17. **Leisure Enough to Spare,** 1360. Yao T'ing-mei (act. 14th century). Handscroll, ink on paper. H. 9 1/16 in. (23 cm.). Detail of colophon, opposite

山復松陰
白晝涼
薜荔芽小
藥譜書
堂怡如
蔣氏
開三徑
不擬荊
人爨五
羊笠弄
偏欣流水
活起行
遠謝世
塵忙展觀
酬富片時
顧恩日致、
暇未遑
乙亥春
御題

18. The Second Coming of the Fifth Patriarch. Yin-t'o-lo (act. ca. mid-14th century). Section of a handscroll mounted as a hanging scroll, ink on paper. H. 12 7/8 in. (32.7 cm.). Detail opposite

19. The Woodcutter of Mount Lo-fou,
1366. Ch'en Ju-yen (act. ca. 1340–ca. 1370).
Hanging scroll, ink on silk. H. 41 3/4 in.
(106 cm.). Detail opposite

至正二十六年正月望後盧山樵
思齊斷事寫羅浮山樵圖
言禱

61

20. Ink Flowers, 1361. Chao Chung (act.
ca. second half of 14th century). Handscroll,
ink on paper. H. 12 1/2 in. (31.9 cm.)

寶帶同心結誓羅衣鈿扁得句錦鴛鴦雙々如是懿
蕭齋窗涛重龍水發香馨君々如是
屈功并題

63

21. Lily and Butterflies. Liu Shan-shou (act. ca. 14th century). Hanging scroll, ink on silk. H. 63 in. (160 cm.). Detail opposite

22. Ramblers Over a Windy Stream.
Lo Chih-ch'uan (act. first half of 14th century). Album leaf, ink on silk. H. 9 9/16 in. (24.3 cm.)

25. Bird on a Prunus Branch. Pien Wen-chin (act. 1413–1427). Album leaf, ink on silk. H. 9 9/16 in. (24.3 cm.)

23. Carrying a Ch'in on a Visit. Artist unknown, late 14th century. Hanging scroll mounted on a panel, ink on silk. H. 31 13/16 in. (80.8 cm.). Detail opposite

蘆花風起浪野
高少雲岩前去
路遠劫外一花
開立不勞脚跟迎
好與蔴條
比丘者敏釋賛

24. Bodhidharma Crossing the Yangtze on a Reed. Artist unknown, 14th century. Hanging scroll, ink on paper. H. 35 1/8 in. (89.2 cm.). Detail opposite

26. Lu Yü's Tea Water Well. Shen Chou
(1427-1509). Album leaf, ink on paper.
H. 12 1/4 in. (31.1 cm.)

27. Thousand-man Seat (or Rock). Shen
Chou (1427–1509). Album leaf, ink on paper.
H. 12 1/4 in. (31.1 cm.)

28. Old Pine Tree. Wen Cheng-ming
(1470–1559). Handscroll, ink on paper.
H. 10 3/4 in. (27.3 cm.)

**31. Taoist Retreat in Mountain and
Stream, Landscape after Ni Tsan,** 1567.
Lu Chih (1496–1576). Hanging scroll, ink
on paper. H. 42 15/16 in. (107.8 cm.).
Detail opposite

32. Mountains on a Clear Autumn Day.
Tung Ch'i-ch'ang (1555–1636). Handscroll,
ink on paper. H. 15 1/8 in. (38.4 cm.).
Detail opposite.

34. Conversation with a Priest, 1643.
Lan Ying (1585–1664). Hanging scroll, ink
on paper. H. 55 7/16 in. (140.8 cm.).
Detail opposite

35. Meditative Visit to a Mountain Retreat, 1648. Hsiang Sheng-mo (1597–1658).
Handscroll, ink on paper. H. 12 in. (30.5 cm.).
Continued overleaf

35. Meditative Visit to a Mountain Retreat. First section of handscroll

38. Landscape in the Style of Wu Chen, 1668. Hsiao Yün-ts'ung (1596–1673). Album leaf, ink on paper. H. 8 1/4 in. (20.9 cm.). Opposite

我愛梅道人落
筆多奇想深
鎪濃染間正似
在林莽 雲岸

36. The Mountains of the Five Cataracts.
Ch'en Hung-shou (1598–1652). Hanging
scroll, ink on silk. H. 46 9/16 in. (118.2 cm.).
Detail opposite

37. Clouds Visiting a Mountain Retreat,
1633. T'ao Hung (act. ca. 1610–1640). Hanging scroll, ink on paper. H. 69 1/2 in. (176.4 cm.). Detail opposite

39. Marshy Landscape. Kung Hsien
(ca. 1620–1689). Album leaf, ink on paper.
H. 12 1/2 in. (31.8 cm.)

41. Landscape after Mi Fei, 1684. Ch'a
Shih-piao (1615–1698). Album leaf, ink
on paper. H. 9 7/16 in. (23.9 cm.)

40. Landscape in the Style of Tung Yüan and Chü-jan, 1650. Kung Hsien (ca. 1620–1689). Hanging scroll, ink on silk. H. 85 3/16 in. (216.3 cm.). Detail opposite

42. Yangtze River Scenery after Huang Kung-wang, 1684. Ch'a Shih-piao (1615–1698). Album leaf, ink on paper. H. 9 7/16 in. (23.9 cm.)

43. Landscape in the Style of Shen Chou, 1690. Mei Ch'ing (1623–1697). Album leaf, ink on paper. H. 11 1/4 in. (28.6 cm.)

44. Landscape in the Style of the Ching-Kuan School, 1690. Mei Ch'ing (1623–1697). Album leaf, ink on paper. H. 11 1/4 in. (28.6 cm.). Detail opposite

45. Fish and Rocks. Chu Ta (1626–1705).
Handscroll, ink on paper. H. 11 1/2 in.
(29.2 cm.)

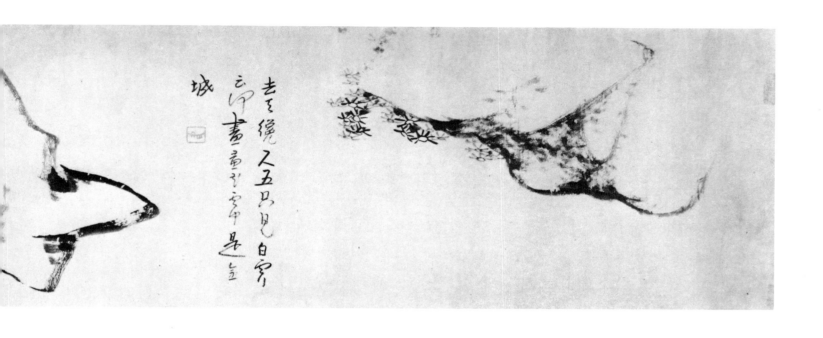

昔文湖州有著霜筍横看宗
思陵題識卷首觀其筆力
不在郭熙之下枝樹間宿葉
竹乃自其肺腑中流出又不
可以筆墨畦徑觀也于文廣
文出希求畫脩竹遠山楷乎
儂之筆力不能倣郭又敢行
彿湖州也我盍若拙林邨野
縱意塗抹聊可以寫一時之
趣姑塞廣文之雅意云
黄鶴山中人王蒙
歲次甲戌九月望後三日為
冒翁先生擬于長安寓齋
海虞 王翬

46. **Tall Bamboo and Distant Mountains
after Wang Meng,** 1694. Wang Hui (1632–
1717). Hanging scroll, ink on paper. H. 31 1/4
in. (79.3 cm.). Detail opposite

104

荊浩自鄴洪谷子乃樵山
水訣一亮嘗謂人曰吳道子
有筆無墨項容有墨無
筆吾當採挹擅探紘而
問谷師之陶户余之冠此係
未任者及居其硯焉

雪嶽詩

47. Landscape with Waterfall. Li Shih-cho (act. 1741–ca. 1765). Hanging scroll, ink on paper. H. 35 7/8 in. (91.1 cm.). Detail opposite

THE GREAT WALL

Chi-ch'iu ●
● Pei-ching

HOPEI

▲ Chü-yang

SHANHSI

▲ Nei-ch'iu

● Chi-nan

SHANTUNG

▲ Tz'u

An-yang ●

YELLOW RIVER
HUANG–HO

KANSU

SHENHSI

▲ Hsiu-wu

Lo-yang ●   Mt. Sung   K'ai-feng ●
▲
Teng-feng

pre 1885
river bed

⚘ Mt. Chung-nan

● Pao-ying

HONAN

CHIANGSU

Nan-ching ●

Ch'ang-shu ●
K'un-shan ●   ● Chia-ting
● Su-chou
● Sung-chiang

ANHUI

Wu-hu ●

Wu-hsing ●   ● Chia-hsing

Hsüan-ch'eng ●

SZECH'UAN

HUPEI

Hang-chou ●

YANGTZE RIVER
CH'ANG–CHIANG

Mt. T'ai-po

Chu-chi ●

Hsiu-ning ●

CHECHIANG

▲
Ching-te-chen ●

● Chiang-shan

Nan-ch'ang ●

Lin-chiang ●

HUNAN

CHIANGHSI

FUCHIEN

KUEICHOU

● Sha-hsien

Te-hua ▲

YÜNNAN

KUANGHSI

KUANGTUNG

Mt. Lou-fu
Nan-hai ●   ● Kuang-chou

Catalogue: Paintings

Explanatory Note

All directions refer to the viewer's frame of reference; thus "left" designates the viewer's left, not that of the painting.

The Wade-Giles system of romanization has been used throughout this catalogue for all words, even geographic and political divisions.

The Cleveland Museum of Art accession numbers appear in each entry.

Information about the seals and colophons appears in the Appendix, beginning on page 134.

Information given under "Published" following the individual catalogue entries is not exhaustive, but is a selected list of the more common and available sources. The abbreviation "Bibl." followed by a number designates a book or magazine listed in the Bibliography.

CMAB refers to *The Cleveland Museum of Art Bulletin.*

The letters *t* and *h* which appear in some catalogue entries, following the name of the artist and followed by other names, stand for *tzu* and *hao*. An explanation of these terms, given in *The Art and Architecture of China*, Laurence Sickman and Alexander Soper (Baltimore, 1960, 2nd ed.), p. 311, states: "*hao*. One of several names chosen by an artist, used in signatures and seals on his paintings. The literary name or sobriquet assumed by an individual. In China the surname (*hsing*) is first, followed by the personal or given name (*ming*). The individual in addition has a courtesy name (*tzu*) which he assumes for general use. Frequently artists take a number of fanciful *hao* or studio names with which they sign their pictures." *Hao* are sometimes derived from the names of home towns and ancestral homes or they may be a quotation from a work of poetry, philosophy, etc.

The map on the facing page shows the major sites mentioned in the catalogue.

1. Buddhist Retreat by Stream and Mountains (*Ch'i-shan lan-jo*)
Attributed to Chü-jan (act. ca. 960–980); from Nan-ching, Chiangsu Province, moved to K'ai-feng, Honan Province
Hanging scroll, ink on silk; H. 73 in. (185.4 cm.), W. 22 5/8 in. (57.5 cm.)
Gift of Katharine Holden Thayer 59.348

The two characters at the top right read "Chü 5" and indicate that this painting is the fifth of a series. Six paintings, entitled *Ch'i-shan lan-jo t'u*, by the monk Chü-jan are recorded in Sung Hui-tsung's (r. 1100–1125) imperial catalogue, *Hsüan-ho Hua-p'u*, and it is likely that this scroll is the fifth of the set. This painting is also recorded in Ch'ing An I-chou's catalogue, *Mo-yüan Hui-kuan*, and Ch'ing Shao Sung-nien's catalogue, *Ku-yüan Ts'ui-lu*, as well as others.

The *lan-jo* of the title is the Chinese word for the Sanskrit *aranya*, which means a forest, and, by extension, an ascetic's hermitage or retreat. The Chinese usage, however, is not as narrow as the Sanskrit. The title of this painting was previously translated as "Buddhist Monastery by Stream and Mountains."

Published: Bibl. 7, pl. 1; Bibl. 10, p. 75a; Bibl. 22, p. 21, no. 13; Bibl. 23, p. 342, fig. 447; Bibl. 35, p. 45, fig. b.

2. Poem by Wang Wei ("Chung-nan pieh-yeh"), 1256
Emperor Li-tsung (r. 1225–1264), named Chao Yün; from Hang-chou, Chechiang Province
Album leaf, ink on silk; H. 9 7/8 in. (25.1 cm.), W. 9 13/16 in. (24.9 cm.)
John L. Severance Fund 61.422

The two lines of poetry, from right to left, read:

> *I walk unto where waters end—*
> *And sit down to watch when clouds arise.*
> (trans. Wai-kam Ho)

This is the penultimate couplet of an eight-line poem, entitled "Chung-nan pieh-yeh," that Wang Wei (699–759) wrote about his villa by the Chung-nan mountain at Wang-ch'uan, Shenhsi Province. This famous poet-painter not only wrote poems about his villa but is also known to have painted a view of the nearby scenery; only copies of that painting are still extant.

This poem and the next album leaf (No. 3) are now part of the album entitled *Scattered Pearls Beyond the Ocean (Hai-wai i-chu).*

Published: Bibl. 24, p. 30, no. 6; Chu Sheng-chai, *Sheng-chai tu-hua-chi* (Hong Kong, 1952), pp. 46–48; Sherman Lee, *Tea Taste in Japanese Art*, exhibition catalogue, Asia House Gallery (New York, 1963), cat. no. 1, ill. p. 11; Lewis and Dorothy Walmsley, *Wang Wei, the Painter Poet* (Tokyo, 1968), p. 144; Tseng Yu-ho Ecke, *Chinese Calligraphy* (Philadelphia, 1971), cat. no. 29 (ill.).

3. Scholar Reclining and Watching Rising Clouds (*Tso-k'an yün-ch'i*), 1256
Ma Lin (act. mid-thirteenth century); from Hang-chou, Chechiang Province
Album leaf, ink and slight color on silk; H. 9 7/8 in. (25.1 cm.), W. 9 15/16 in. (25.3 cm.)
John L. Severance Fund 61.421

This leaf, signed in the lower left "Your subject, Ma Lin" (Ch'en Ma Lin), illustrates the Wang Wei poem in the imperial calligraphy by Li-tsung (No. 2), and it is from the relationship of these two album leaves that the date 1256 is ascertained. A particular cyclical date occurs once every sixty years; and since this album leaf and the preceding leaf, dated *ping-ch'en*, were originally mounted together (which was determined by measuring the holes resulting from their having been actually mounted on a fan), the year *ping-ch'en* during Ma Lin's life must be the year 1256, and the imperial seals must be those of the Emperor Li-tsung.

Published: Bibl. 24, p. 31, no. 6; Bibl. 28, p. 321, ill. 60; Bibl. 43, p. 23, no. 35; Chu Sheng-chai, *Sheng-chai tu-hua-chi*, pp. 46–48; Lee, *Tea Taste in Japanese Art*, cat. no. 1, ill. p. 13.

4. Dragon (*Lung t'u*)
Attributed to Mu Ch'i (act. mid-thirteenth century), *h.* Fa-ch'ang; from Szech'uan Province, moved to Ch'ien-t'ang (Hang-chou) and the Liu-t'ung Monastery of West Lake, Chechiang Province
Hanging scroll, ink on silk; H. 48 3/4 in. (123.8 cm.), W. 22 in. (55.9 cm.)
Purchase from the J. H. Wade Fund 58.427

The dragon is a complex symbol and its meaning varies according to time and place. Generally speaking, the dragon as guardian of the waters and clouds is inextricably linked with the elements necessary for fertile agriculture. In Chinese literature, the dragon has been described as having the horns of a stag, head of a camel, eyes of a demon, neck of a snake, belly of a sea monster, scales of a carp, claws of an eagle, pads of a tiger, and ears of an ox (see Bibl. 46, p. 186). It is the masculine animal, the animal of the East.

Published: Bibl. 2, p. 62, no. 28; Bibl. 21, p. 5, fig. 6; Bibl. 30, p. 249, cat. no. 24b; Bibl. 34, cat. no. 3b, pl. V; *CMAB* (November 1972), p. 241, fig. 3.

5. Tiger (*Hu t'u*)
Attributed to Mu Ch'i (act. mid-thirteenth century), *h.* Fa-ch'ang; from Szech'uan Province, moved to Ch'ien-t'ang (Hang-chou) and the Liu-t'ung Monastery of West Lake, Chechiang Province
Hanging scroll, ink and slight color on silk; H. 48 3/4 in. (123.8 cm.), W. 22 in. (55.9 cm.)
Purchase from the J. H. Wade Fund 58.428

With the dragon scroll (No. 4), this forms a pair of hanging scrolls, the motif of which dates back to ancient times. Scrolls such as these were used to decorate the walls of official buildings, and they were almost as numerous as portraits. The tiger means much the same thing as it does in the Occident; for example, it symbolizes bravery. It is also complementary to the dragon in that it watches over the earth and mountains and is the female animal, the animal of the West.

Published: Bibl. 2, p. 62, no. 27; Bibl. 21, p. 5, fig. 4; Bibl. 30, p. 249, cat. no. 24b; Bibl. 34, cat. no. 3a, pl. IV; Bibl. 35, p. 61, fig. D; *CMAB* (November 1972), p. 241, fig. 2.

6. Shakyamuni Coming Down from the Mountains (*Shih-chia ch'u-shan*), 1244
Artist unknown
Hanging scroll, ink on paper; H. 29 3/8 in. (74.6 cm.), W. 12 13/16 in. (32.6 cm.)
John L. Severance Fund 70.2

The poem by Ch'ih-chüeh Tao-ch'ung reads:

> *Since entering the mountain, too dried out and emaciated*
> *Frosty cold over the snow,*
> *After having a twinkling of revelation with impassioned eyes*
> *Why then do you want to come back to the world?*
> *(The second day of the eighth month in the* chia-ch'en *year of the reign*
> *Ch'un-yu* [1244], *Tao-ch'ung, resident of T'ai-po mountain.)*
> (trans. Wai-kam Ho)

This painting is the earliest known dated representation of a famous moment in the life of Shakyamuni, the historic Buddha. Shakyamuni left his royal home and spent six years in search of enlightenment. During that time he practiced an extremely ascetic life in the wilderness, torturing his body and eating but a kernel of corn once every two weeks. Realizing that all was in vain, he stopped what he was doing, came down from the mountains, and resumed a normal life. Soon thereafter he achieved enlightenment and became the Buddha.

Published: Bibl. 28, p. 317, ill. 56; Bibl. 37, p. 150, ill. 6; *CMAB* (November 1972), p. 241, fig. 1.

7. Returning Birds and Old Cypress (*Ku-po Kuei-ch'in*)
Artist unknown, Sung dynasty
Album leaf, ink on silk; H. 9 3/8 in. (23.8 cm.), W. 9 13/16 in. (24.9 cm.)
Gift of Dr. and Mrs. Sherman E. Lee 69.305

The use of various sobriquets (see Explanatory Note) was a prevalent Chinese custom, especially among the literati. Sobriquets are particularly noticeable in the seal inscriptions of artists, collectors, officials, etc. The one given in the seal on the lower left of the painting is not unique; thus a definitive identification of the artist cannot be made.

Published: Bibl. 43, p. 18, cat. no. 24.

8. Waterfall (*Yin-yen fei-p'u*)
Artist unknown, late Sung to early Yüan dynasties
Hanging scroll, ink on silk; H. 33 in. (83.8 cm.), W. 14 3/8 in. (36.5 cm.)
Gift of Mary B. Lee, C. Bingham Blossom, Dudley S. Blossom III, Laurel B. Kovacik, and Elizabeth B. Blossom in memory of Elizabeth B. Blossom 72.157

In the title, written by a Mr. T'ang of Pi-ling, Chiangsu Province (three of whose seals appear on the painting), the artist is said to be Chiang Shen (*t.* Kuan-tao, act. first half of the twelfth century), but this attribution cannot be sustained.

Published: *CMAB* (March 1973), ill. 327, p. 97.

9. Bodhidharma Meditating Facing a Cliff (*Ta-mo mien-pi*)
Artist unknown, late thirteenth century
Hanging scroll, ink on silk; H. 45 3/4 in. (116.2 cm.), W. 18 1/4 in. (46.3 cm.)
John L. Severance Fund 72.41

Bodhidharma (in Japanese, Daruma; died ca. A.D. 530), the twenty-eighth Indian patriarch and founder of the Chinese Ch'an sect of Buddhism (in Japanese, Zen), is the first Chinese patriarch. Legend has it that this prince from southern India came into China through Kuang-chou, Kuang-tung Province (Canton) in the first quarter of the sixth century. After crossing the Yangtze River on a reed (see No. 24), he spent nine years meditating before the cliff at the Shao-lin temple of Mt. Sung near Lo-yang, Honan Province. It was during this time that Hui-k'o (ca. 487–593), who was to become the second Ch'an patriarch, went to seek instruction from Bodhidharma; he is seen here approaching the master. Hui-k'o is said to have cut off his own arm and presented it to Bodhidharma as proof of his sincerity and resolve to study with the master. This picture seems to represent an encounter prior to that event.

Published: Previous publications have attributed this painting to Yen Tz'u-p'ing. Bibl. 13, pl. 136; Bibl. 33, vol. II, p. 89; Bibl. 38, pl. 72; Asahi shimbun-sha [Asahi newspaper company], Special Issue for the *To-Sō-Gen-Mei meiga-ten go* (December 1928), ill. p. 32; *CMAB* (November 1972), pp. 241–44, fig. 4.

10. Bamboos, Rocks, and Lonely Orchids (*Chu shih yu-lan*)
Chao Meng-fu (1254–1322), *t.* Tzu-ang, *h.* Sung-hsüeh; from Wu-hsing, Chechiang Province

Handscroll, ink on paper; H. 19 7/8 in. (50.5 cm.), L. 56 3/4 in. (144.1 cm.)
John L. Severance Fund, by exchange 63.515

The artist's inscription at the lower left reads, "Meng-fu drew this for Shan-fu." At the upper right, the artist inscribed the title of the painting. One seal of the artist follows the inscription (Chao Tzu-ang shih), and two others appear on the left corners (Sung-hsüeh-chai; T'ien-shui-chün t'u-shu-yin).

The painting bears many seals and colophons (see Appendix). The colophon by Han Hsing (1266-1341) reads:

Those ancients who excelled in calligraphy were also always good in painting. Even a random drop of ink turned into a housefly [like the early sixth-century artist Chang Seng-yu] would be full of life, be- fitting the object. These orchids and rocks by the venerable master Sung-hsüeh embrace both the brush method of the "running" style as well as the "flying white" manner in calligraphy. Indeed, it should be treasured. [signed] Han Hsing of An-yang. [Bibl. 26]

The colophon by Chao I, son of Meng-fu, reads:

Chih-cheng, eleventh year [1351], tenth moon, twenty-eighth day, [your] son, I, after paying respects, carefully examined [this]. [Bibl. 26]

The colophon by Ch'en Chi (1314-1370) reads:

On seeing the Bamboos, Rocks, and Lonely Orchids by the Duke from Wu-hsing, Chao Meng-fu, one feels one is suddenly cleansed of his lowly and narrow-minded sentiments. His brush moves so freely at his will, vertically and horizontally [as though meeting no resistance]. It comes so naturally with a disarming flair of naiveté and earnestness, as though coming directly from the calligraphies of the two Wangs [Wang Hsi-chih, 321-371, and his son Wang Hsien-chih, 344-388]. No wonder it has been so much more treasured and enjoyed by Chung-ying [Ku Te-hui, or Ku Ying, 1310-1369] than any other ordinary works. Written on the tenth day of the fourth month of the eighth year of Chih-cheng [1348]. [signed] Ch'en Chi of T'ien-t'ai. [Bibl. 26]

For a reconstruction of the history of this painting, a clarification of some discrepancies, and the reason for limiting the date to Chao Meng-fu's residence in the capital, Pei-ching, Hopei Province (1286-1292 or 1314-1319), see Bibl. 26.

Published: Bibl. 10, p. 395; Bibl. 17, pl. 94; Bibl. 26, cat. no. 235 (ill.); Bibl. 27, p. 58, ill. 34; Bibl. 33, vol. VII, p. 104; Liang Chang-chu, *Tui-An chin-shih shu-hua pa* [Notes on Calligraphy, Painting, and Inscriptions on Bronzes and Stone] (1855), vol. XIII, p. 5; Wu Ch'i-chen, *Shu-hua-chi* [Notes on Calligraphy and Painting] (Shanghai, 1963 reprint), ch. 6, p. 638; *CMAB* (November 1972), p. 247, fig. 8 (detail).

11. Old Trees by a Cool Spring (*Ch'ing-ch'üan ch'iao-mu*), 1326
Li Shih-hsing (1282-1328), t. Tsun-tao, h. Hsi-shan-tao-jen; from Chi-ch'iu, Hopei Province
Hanging scroll, ink on silk; H. 65 1/4 in. (165.7 cm.), W. 42 3/4 in. (108.6 cm.)
Purchase, J. H. Wade Fund 70.41

The artist's inscription at the left edge reads, "In the twelfth month of winter, in the *ping-yin* year of the reign T'ai-ting [1326], Li Shih-hsing, Tsun-tao, of Chi-ch'iu did this." Three seals of the artist follow (Li Shih-hsing yin; Li Tsun-tao shih; Yu-hsi-han-mo).

This painting should not be confused with the similar undated work by the same artist, entitled *The Guardians of the Valley*, in the Fogg Art Museum, Harvard University, which has been published in Bibl. 22, p. 43, Fig. 30, and Bibl. 26, no. 225.

12. Poetic Feeling in a Thatched Pavilion (*Ts'ao-t'ing shih-i*), 1347
Wu Chen (1280-1354), t. Chung-kuei, h. Mei-hua-tao-jen; from Chia-hsing, Chechiang Province
Handscroll, ink on paper; H. 9 3/8 in. (23.8 cm.), L. 39 1/8 in. (99.4 cm.)
Purchase, Leonard C. Hanna Jr. Bequest 63.259

The artist's poem and inscription at the left end read:

By the side of the hamlet I built a thatched pavilion. Balanced and squared, it is lofty in conception. The woods being deep, birds are happy; the dust being distant, bamboos and pines are clean. Streams and rocks invite lingering enjoyment, lutes and books please my temperament. How should I bid farewell to the world of the ordinary and the familiar, and let my heart go its own way for the gratification of my life?
In the tenth month of winter, in ting-hai, *the seventh year of Chih-cheng [1347], I did this* Poetic Feeling in a Thatched Pavilion *playfully for Yüan-tse. Written by Mei sha-mi [Novice of the Plum Blossom]. [Bibl. 26]*

Following this inscription are two seals of the artist (Mei-hua-an; Chia-hsing Wu Chen Chung-kuei shu-hua-chi).
The colophon by Shen Chou (1427-1509) reads:

I love the Old Man of the Plum-blossom,
Who inherited the secrets of Chü-jan from heart to heart.*
In cultivating this "water and ink kinship"
He was able to endow everything with a touch of aged mellowness.
Trees and rocks seem to fall from his brush [so effortlessly]
That even nature itself could hardly deny their emergence.
So now, under the grove of the oak trees,
I am willing to serve him with all humility.
[signed] Shen Chou, a later follower. [Bibl. 26]

Published: Bibl. 10, p. 105b; Bibl. 25, p. 3, fig. 1; Bibl. 26, cat. no. 252 (ill.); Chang Ch'ou, *Ch'ing-ho shu-hua-fang* [The Ch'ing-ho Boat-Studio of Painting and Calligraphy, reedited by Wen Hsiu] (Hsin-min Book Co., 1876 reprint), ch. 7, p. 48b; Chang Ch'ou, *Chen-chi jih-lu* [Daily Notes on Authentic Works] (ca. 1900 reprint), vol. I, p. 55b; Pien Yung-yü, *Shih-ku-t'ang shu-hua hui-k'ao* [Pien's Notes and Records on Calligraphies and Paintings] (Shanghai, 1921 reprint), ch. 19, pp. 1a-2a; Wang K'o-yü, *San-hu-wang* [Netted Corals] (Shanghai, 1934 reprint), ch. 9, p. 919; *Seize peintures de maîtres Chinois XIIe-XVIIIe siècles, collection Chiang Er-shih* (Paris, 1959), cat. no. 2 (ill.); Chu Sheng-chai, *Chung-kuo shu-hua* [Illustrated Album of Chinese Calligraphies and Paintings] (Hong Kong, 1961), vol. I, fig. 5; Ku Fu, *P'ing-sheng-chuang-kuan* [Records on Calligraphies and Paintings] (Shanghai, 1962 reprint), ch. 9, p. 62.

*The monk Chü-jan and the "follower" Shen Chou are represented by Nos. 1 and 26, 27, respectively.

13. Travelers in Autumn Mountains (*Ch'iu-shan hsing-lu*)
Sheng Mou (act. first half of fourteenth century), t. Tzu-chao; from Chia-hsing, Chechiang Province
Album leaf, ink on silk; H. 9 5/8 in. (24.4 cm.), W. 10 7/16 in. (26.5 cm.)
Mr. and Mrs. Severance A. Millikin Collection 63.589

In the upper right corner, the original signature of the artist has been scraped away, so that only the character "Sheng" of his last name is legible.

Published: Bibl. 24, p. 35, no. 10; Bibl. 26, cat. no. 232 (ill.); Bibl. 30, cat. no. 31, pp. 54-55 (ill.); Bibl. 35, pp. 69-70, ill. p. 182; Bibl. 43, p. 28, no. 49.

14. The Lantern Night Excursion of Chung K'uei (*Chung K'uei yüan-yeh ch'u-yu*)

Yen Hui (act. first half of fourteenth century), *t.* Ch'iu-yüeh; from Chiang-shan, Chechiang Province
Handscroll, ink on silk; H. 9 3/4 in. (24.8 cm.), L. 94 5/8 in. (240.3 cm.)
Mr. and Mrs. William H. Marlatt Fund 61.206

There are various legends surrounding the person of Chung K'uei, the demon-killer, who is represented here on a New Year's night. A current popular one states that during the Wu-te reign (618–626) of the T'ang Emperor Kao-tsu, Chung K'uei placed first in the imperial examinations (perhaps the *chin-shih*-level, equivalent to a doctorate in the West). Because of his shame at being rejected by the Emperor (some say this was the result of Chung's extreme ugliness; others say he was unjustly defrauded), Chung K'uei committed suicide. Later, the T'ang Emperor Ming Huang (Hsüan-tsung, r. 712–756) dreamed of Chung K'uei, dressed in a tattered official's robe, protecting him from the evil spirit Hsü Hao. Upon awakening, the Emperor ordered the famous painter Wu Tao-tzu to paint Chung's portrait—which he did to perfection. Wu's painting of Chung K'uei survived until the Sung period; it was recorded in the collection of the Emperor Hui-tsung (r. 1101–1125).

Published: Bibl. 10, p. 454b; Bibl. 26, cat. no. 206 (ill.); Bibl. 30, cat. no. 27, pp. 46–47 (ill.); Bibl. 33, vol. VII, p. 144; Wang K'o-yü, *San-hu-wang*, ch. 9, pp. 927–36; Michael Sullivan, "Chinese Art Under the Mongols," *Apollo*, vol. LXXXVII, ill. p. 261; *CMAB* (February 1962), pp. 36–41, figs. 1, 3, 4.

15. The Nine Songs (*Chiu-ko-t'u*), 1360
Chang Wu (act. 1335–1365), *t.* Shu-hou, *h.* Chen-ch'i-sheng; from Hang-chou, Chechiang Province
Handscroll, ink on paper; H. 11 in. (27.9 cm.), L. 172 1/2 in. (438 cm.)
Purchase, J. H. Wade Fund 59.138

The text of each of the songs is to the left of each section of the painting and was written in *li-shu* (clerical script) by Ch'u Huan (act. mid-fourteenth century). *The Nine Songs*, or hymns (actually eleven in number), are ascribed with varying qualifications to Ch'ü Yüan (ca. 340–ca. 280 B.C.). Ch'ü Yüan, author of the similarly famous *Li-sao*, is regarded as a model of good behavior among officials. Completely disillusioned by the corruption in the government of the Ch'u state, from which he was banished, he drowned himself in the Mi-lo River on the "fifth day of the fifth month." The famous Dragon Boat Festival, still celebrated today, commemorates this event.

The Nine Songs, though enigmatic, are very important for understanding the culture of the Ch'u state, since they are the songs or hymns that the priests and priestesses used in the ceremonies of Ch'ü Yüan's time. It is perhaps because of this function that the songs' exact meanings and implications are still debated by scholars. Some English translations can be found in Arthur Waley's *Nine Songs* (London, 1955) and Kojiro Tomita's article "Scroll of 'The Nine Songs' of Ch'ü Yüan," *Bulletin of the Boston Museum of Fine Arts* (October 1937), which illustrates a version in that museum with interesting compositional and figural changes and variations.

Published: Bibl. 6, p. 138; Bibl. 9, p. 216, no. 785; Bibl. 12, figs. 10, 11; Bibl. 26, cat. no. 187 (ill.); Bibl. 30, cat. no. 36, pp. 62–63 (ill.); Bibl. 33, vol. VI, pls. 44, 45; Bibl. 33, vol. VII, p. 100; Lu Shih-hua, *Wu-Yüeh-so-chien shu-hua-lu* [Calligraphies and Paintings Seen in the Chiangsu-Chechiang Area] (Shanghai, 1910 reprint), vol. III, pp. 6a–6b; Cheng Chen-to, ed., *Ch'u-tz'u-t'u* [Illustrations for the *Songs of Ch'u*] (Peking, 1953): vol. I, pls. 7–9, is a late copy of The Cleveland Museum of Art painting;

Chung-kuo ku-tai-hui-hua hsüan-chi [Selected Paintings of the Past] (Peking, 1963), pl. 63; Richard Barnhart, "Survival, Revivals, and the Classical Tradition of Chinese Figure Painting," *Proceedings of the International Symposium on Chinese Painting*, National Palace Museum, June 1970 (Taipei, 1972), p. 174, ill. 21, p. 140.

16. Bamboo in the Wind (*Feng-chu*)
P'u Ming (act. mid-fourteenth century), *h.* Hsüeh-ch'uang, family name Ts'ao; from Sung-chiang, Chiangsu Province
Hanging scroll, ink on silk; H. 30 in. (76.2 cm.), W. 17 5/8 in. (44.8 cm.)
John L. Severance Fund 53.246   *ill. p. 47*

At the left edge of the painting are the artist's signature and two of his seals (Hsüeh-ch'uang).

Published: Bibl. 9, cat. no. 788, ill. p. 217; Bibl. 13, p. 397; Bibl. 26, cat. no. 244 (ill.); Bibl. 33, vol. VII, p. 129; *Kokka* 424 (March 1926), p. 73, pl. 5; Lee, *Tea Taste in Japanese Art*, cat. no. 6, ill. p. 20; *CMAB* (February 1956), pp. 22–24, ill. p. 18; *CMAB* (November 1972), p. 247, fig. 7.

17. Leisure Enough to Spare (*Yu-yü-hsien t'u*), 1360
Yao T'ing-mei (act. fourteenth century); from Wu-hsing, Chechiang Province
Handscroll, ink on paper; H. 9 1/16 in. (23 cm.), L. 33 1/16 in. (84 cm.)
John L. Severance Fund 54.791

At the left, following the painting, are the artist's inscription and poem, which read:

> In the first month of spring in the twentieth year of the reign of Chih-cheng [1360], I painted this and attached a few rustic words at the end of the scroll.
> The place is remote and people far away.
> The wooden gate is kept closed always,
> The courtyard is covered by the pine shade,
> Daytime passes by idly.
> Thus you may well forget the wind and dust in your eyes,
> And look at the flowing waters only while at ease,
> And at the distant mountains, lying down.
>   [signed] Yao T'ing-mei of Wu-hsing. [Bibl. 26]

It is thought that the painting and some of the contemporary poems and colophons, including an essay by Yang Wei-cheng (1296–1370) on "Leisure to Spare," commemorate a gathering of scholars held at the villa of one of the poets in 1359. Probably this group paid a visit to the hermit Tu, portrayed in the painting, who lived nearby and whose idyllic life is described by Yang Wei-cheng. (For further information, see Bibl. 26, no. 260.)

Published: Bibl. 5, pls. 40–47; Bibl. 10, p. 187a; Bibl. 19, p. 147, no. 34; Bibl. 22, p. 53, ill. 37; Bibl. 23, p. 414, fig. 548; Bibl. 26, cat. no. 260 (ill.); Bibl. 33, vol. VII, p. 144; Ch'en Jen-t'ao, *Chin-kuei lün-hua* [Essays on Chinese Painting] (Hong Kong, 1956), p. 64; Ch'en Jen-t'ao, *Ku-kung i-i shu-hua-mu chiao-chu* [An Annotated List of the Lost Calligraphies and Paintings from the (Ch'ing) Palace Collection] (Hong Kong, 1956), p. 15b; Wu Ch'i-chen, *Shu-hua-chi* [Notes on Calligraphy and Painting] (Shanghai, 1963 reprint), ch. 3, pp. 272–73.

18. The Second Coming of the Fifth Patriarch (*Wu-tsu tsai-lai t'u*)
Yin-t'o-lo (act. ca. mid-fourteenth century), *t.* Jen-fan; active in Pien-liang (K'ai-feng), Honan Province
Section of a handscroll mounted as a hanging scroll, ink on paper; H. 12 7/8 in. (32.7 cm.), W. 17 9/16 in. (45.6 cm.)
Purchase, J.H. Wade Fund 67.211

The partial artist's seal at the lower left corner can be reconstructed and reads:

People say in the Immortal's grottoes the peach blossoms are blooming in the warmth of spring. I wonder if such flowering branches ever exist in our world. [Bibl. 26]

The poem by Ch'u-shih Fan-ch'i reads:

This boy has no father, only a mother,
Master of Ch'an, please don't ask him when he was born—
The green pine is not yet old, and the yellow plum is ripe.
Two lives are but like fleeting moments of a dream.

(trans. Wai-kam Ho)

This translation differs slightly from the one published earlier (Bibl. 26, no. 208).

Hung-jen (602–675), the Fifth Patriarch, was an abbot's attendant in his previous life. After his transmigration, he was immaculately conceived by a woman named Chou from Hupei Province. He and his mother became beggars after they were thrown out by her parents. Here Yin-t'o-lo has probably depicted Chou and her child, Hung-jen, meeting the Fourth Patriarch and his attendant.

Published: Bibl. 16, ill. pp. 126, 127; Bibl. 26, cat. no. 208 (ill.); Bibl. 28, p. 317, ill. 57; Inoue Seisan, ed., *Daibei* [The Great Beauty] (Osaka, 1960), cat. no. 6 (ill.); *CMAB* (November 1972), pp. 245–47, fig. 6.

19. The Woodcutter of Mount Lo-fou (*Lo-fou-shan-ch'iao*), 1366
Ch'en Ju-yen (act. ca. 1340–1370), *t.* Wei-yün, *h.* Ch'iu-shui; from Su-chou, Chiangsu Province, moved to Chi-nan, Shantung Province
Hanging scroll, ink on silk; H. 41 3/4 in. (106 cm.), W. 21 in. (53.3 cm.)
Mr. and Mrs. A. Dean Perry Collection

The artist's inscription in the upper left corner reads:

In the twenty-sixth year of Chih-cheng [1366], the first month after the fifteenth day, Ch'en Ju-yen of Lu-shan painted this Woodcutter of Mount Lo-fou *for Ssu-ch'i, the Judge.*

In his colophon on this painting, Huang Jen (see Appendix) suggests that the woodcutter portrayed here may well be the Taoist immortal Ko Hung (283–343, *t.* Chih-ch'uan). Ko Hung is inextricably linked with the alchemical aspect of Taoism (the religion, not the philosophy, is being considered here). His *Pao-p'o-tzu*, a virtual compendium of decoctions and alchemical terminology, is one of the first and most famous books on the subject. Ko Hung came from a very poor family in Chiangsu Province, and it is said that he had to chop and sell firewood in order to pay for the paper and ink necessary for his studies. He studied alchemy and medicine in his youth and had a fairly successful official career, but he did not like that life. When he heard where important ingredients for the elixir of immortality could be found, he asked to have his post transferred to that locale. Ko Hung thus moved his home, taking his wife and children with him. On his way through Kuang-chou, he became a recluse in the Lo-fou mountains, devoted himself to alchemy, and found the elixir of immortality.

In this work, the artist Ch'en Ju-yen, from the same province as Ko Hung, has painted a woodcutter in the Lo-fou mountains carrying, among other things, a calabash or double gourd, a popular Taoist symbol. Though not so specified in the artist's inscription, the woodcutter is probably meant to represent Ko Hung.

Published: Bibl. 5, pl. 51; Bibl. 10, p. 296; Bibl. 22, p. 140, no. 38; Bibl. 26, cat. no. 265 (ill.); Bibl. 30, no. 40a, p. 254; Bibl. 33, vol. VI, pl. 112; Bibl. 33, vol. VII, p. 165; Bibl. 42, no. 8; Ku Fu, *P'ing-sheng-chuang-kuan*, ch. 9, pp. 116, 117.

20. Ink Flowers (*Mo-hua*), 1361
Chao Chung (act. ca. second half of fourteenth century), *t.* Yüan-ch'u, *h.* Tung-wu-yeh-jen; from Wu-chiang (Su-chou), Chiangsu Province
Handscroll, ink on paper; H. 12 1/2 in. (31.9 cm.), L. 60 5/16 in. (153.1 cm.)
John L. Severance Fund 67. 36

Each flower in this painting is accompanied by a poem signed by the artist. One artist's seal follows the first poem (Chao Chung yüan-ch'u hua-chi), and two seals follow the second poem. The artist's inscription at the left end of the scroll reads:

I did this scroll using T'ang Cheng-chung's method of "ink-flower painting." I also composed poems in the style of Li Ho in praise of these flowers. My poems and paintings may not be very good; they are nonetheless all derived from the heritage of the ancients. It is just as if one wants to draw a square or circle, one must first know how to use the ruler and the compass. May the connoisseur kindly refrain from laughing at them. The fifteenth day of the eighth month in the hsin-ch'ou *year of the reign Chih-cheng [1361]. Respectfully inscribed by Tung-Wu-yeh-jen [a rustic of the Eastern Wu], Chao Chung, Yüan-ch'u.* [Bibl. 26]

Following the inscription are two seals of the artist (Chao Yüan-ch'u; Ch'uan-shih-ch'ing-wan).

The painter T'ang Cheng-chung, mentioned above, is said to have followed the style of his uncle Yang Pu-chih (1097–1169) and to have exploited the contrasts of black and white in his painting of ink prunus (plum blossoms). Yang Pu-chih is famous for his "village, or wild, prunus" (*ts'un yeh mei*), painted on paper—in a style which was less luxuriant, plump, and idealistic than the Academy-style "palace prunus" (*kung mei*). *Wen Wu*, no. 1, 1973, has a discussion and illustration of Yang Pu-chih's *Ssu-mei-hua t'u* (Four Prunus Flowers).

Li Ho (790–816), also mentioned in the inscription, was a T'ang dynasty poet who, tradition says, began to write at the age of six.

Published: Bibl. 1, vol. XXII, p. 109, fig. 10; Bibl. 17, pl. 107; Bibl. 26, cat. no. 183 (ill.); Asahi shimbun-sha, Special Issue for the *To-Sō-Gen-Mei meiga-ten go* (December 1928), ill. p. 42.

21. Lily and Butterflies (*Hsüan-tieh t'u*)
Liu Shan-shou (act. ca. fourteenth century)
Hanging scroll, ink on silk; H. 63 in. (160 cm.), W. 23 in. (58.4 cm.)
Purchase, J. H. Wade Fund 71.132

On the middle right of the painting the artist has written the title and affixed three seals, only two of which can be deciphered (Liu Shan-shou; Shou-chai).

Published: *CMAB* (January 1972), p. 45, no. 132, ill. p. 32 (the painting was incorrectly recorded as being on paper).

22. Ramblers Over a Windy Stream (*Hsi-chao ts'e-chang*)
Lo Chih-ch'uan (act. first half of fourteenth century); from Yü-ch'uan (Lin-chiang), Chianghsi Province
Album leaf, ink on silk; H. 9 9/16 in. (24.3 cm.), W. 9 7/8 in. (25.1 cm.)
Gift of John Huntington Art and Polytechnic Trust 15.536

On the lower left of the painting, the artist's seal (Chih-ch'uan) is partially obliterated but readable.

Published: Bibl. 24, p. 36, no. 11; Bibl. 26, cat. no. 215 (ill.); Bibl. 43, p. 30, cat. no. 55, ill. p. 59.

23. Carrying a Ch'in on a Visit (*Hsieh-ch'in fang-yu t'u*)
Artist unknown, late fourteenth century
Hanging scroll mounted on a panel, ink on silk; H. 31 13/16 in. (80.8 cm.),
W. 13 7/8 in. (35.2 cm.)
Purchase, General Income Fund 19.974

This painting was previously entitled *Landscape.* It is in the style of
Li Ch'eng (act. 960–990) and Kuo Hsi (ca. 1020–ca. 1075), two Northern
Sung dynasty masters from North China.

Published: Bibl. 26, cat. no 218 (ill.).

24. Bodhidharma Crossing the Yangtze on a Reed (*Ta-mo i-wei
tu-chiang*)
Artist unknown, fourteenth century
Hanging scroll, ink on paper; H. 35 1/8 in. (89.2 cm.), W. 12 1/4 in.
(31.1 cm.)
John L. Severance Fund 64.44

The poem by the priest Liao-an Ch'ing-yü reads:

> *Wind rises from the reed flowers, the waves are high,*
> *It's a long way to go beyond the cliff of the Shao-shih mountain,*
> *Above the worlds of kalpas a flower is opening into five petals,*
> *So that your barefoot heels are just fine for the whipping rattans.*
> [Bibl. 26]

In Buddhist cosmology, a "kalpa" is the amount of time it takes the
universe to undergo one cycle of creation and destruction. A great kalpa
is 1,344,000,000 years. The "whipping rattans" in the poem's last line is a
reference to the way in which a teacher kept kneeling students awake—
by striking them on the arches of their bare feet.
      According to legend, Bodhidharma, the first Chinese patriarch,
crossed the Yangtze River on a reed after his audience with the Liang
dynasty Emperor Wu-ti (r. 502–549). This event preceded his arrival at
the Shao-lin monastery, where he meditated for nine years (see No. 9).
The monastery, built in A.D. 496, is in northwest Teng-feng-hsien, Honan
Province, north of the Shao-shih mountain alluded to in the poem. Some
stories relate that Bodhidharma cut off his eyelids while meditating there
in order to make sleeping impossible; others say that his eyelids atrophied
from disuse. It is perhaps because of this famous trait that he is often pic-
tured with a distinctive, glaring visage, even in scenes such as the one
represented here, which actually predate his nine-year meditation.

Published: Bibl. 26, cat. no. 209 (ill.); Lee, *Tea Taste in Japanese Art,*
cat. no. 3, ill. p. 17; *CMAB* (November 1972), pp. 241–43, fig. 5.

25. Bird on a Prunus Branch (*Han-ch'üeh t'u*)
Pien Wen-chin (act. 1413–1427), *t.* Ching-chao; from Sha-hsien, Fuchien
Province, moved to Pei-ching, Hopei Province
Album leaf, ink on silk; H. 9 9/16 in. (24.3 cm.), W. 8 1/4 in. (21 cm.)
Gift of Dr. and Mrs. Sherman E. Lee 67.249   *ill. p. 67*

The artist's inscription in the upper left corner reads: "Painted by Pien
Ching-chao of Lung-hsi, painter-in-attendance *(tai-chao)* of Wu-ying-tien."
Over this are two seals of the artist (I-ch'ing-tung-chih; Pien Wen-chin
shih).
      Though reference sources state that Pien Wen-chin came from Sha-
hsien, the viewer should not be confused by the fact that Lung-hsi (another
name for Kansu Province) is indicated as the artist's "home" in this inscription. The Pien family's ancestral home was Lung-hsi, so Pien
Wen-chin's reference to this place is not unusual. Likewise, in No. 10,
one of the seals used by Chao Meng-fu (T'ien-shui-chün t'u-shu-yin) refers

to T'ien-shui in Kansu Province, the ancestral home of the Chao family
(of the Sung dynasty imperial clan), to which the artist was related; yet
Chao Meng-fu was actually from Wu-hsing, Chechiang Province.

26. Lu Yü's Tea Water Well (*Lu Yü ch'a-ching*)
Shen Chou (1427–1509), *t.* Ch'i-nan, *h.* Shih-t'ien; from Su-chou,
Chiangsu Province
Album leaf, ink on paper; H. 12 1/4 in. (31.1 cm.), W. 15 13/16 in.
(40.1 cm.)
Leonard C. Hanna Jr. Bequest 64.371d

A seal of the artist (Ch'i-nan) is at the lower right corner of the painting.
This is the fourth leaf of a twelve-leaf album entitled *Twelve Views of
Tiger Hill (Hu-ch'iu-shan)* by Shen Chou. For a translation of the colophon
by Yao Yüan-chih (1776–1852) that accompanies this album, see Bibl. 25.
      Tiger Hill (130 Sung feet high) is just outside of Su-chou in Wu
county, Chiangsu Province. It is called Sea Crest Hill (Hai-yung-shan)
and has been called Martial Hill (Wu-ch'iu). It is said that Ho Lung, king
of the Wu state (r. 514–489 B.C.), was buried there and that a white tiger
crouched on his grave for three days; thus the local inhabitants named
the spot Tiger Hill.
      "Lu Yü's tea water well" is located above the "Nodding Stone" (see
No. 27); it is also known as the "World's Third Spring." The well is famous
for the coldness of its water. Lu Yü (d. 804) is traditionally credited with
being the author of the *Ch'a Ching (Tea Classic),* though this attribution is
not without question (see Bibl. 29, p. x).

Published: This painting was previously entitled "Drought Demon
Spring." Bibl. 12, fig. 60; Bibl. 19, ill. p. 76; Bibl. 20, pp. 473–76, pl. 5,
fig. 7; Bibl. 22, pp. 67–68, ill. 52; Bibl. 25, pp. 4–7, fig. 11; Bibl. 33, vol.
VII, p. 229.

27. Thousand-man Seat (or Rock) (*Ch'ien-jen-tso* [or *shih*])
Shen Chou (1427–1509), *t.* Ch'i-nan, *h.* Shih-t'ien; from Su-chou,
Chiangsu Province
Album leaf, ink on paper; H. 12 1/4 in. (31.1 cm.), W. 15 13/16 in.
(40.2 cm.)
Leonard C. Hanna Jr. Bequest 64.371b

At the lower left corner of the painting is one seal of the artist (Ch'i-nan).
This leaf is from the album entitled *Twelve Views of Tiger Hill* (see No. 26).
      The thousand-man seat (or rock) is recorded to be a huge, platelike
rock, which can seat a thousand men, at the end of the road leading to
Tiger Hill. In the northeast corner is a small stone pagoda, called the Indra
Pagoda (Chin-kang-t'a), and on it is carved the Diamond Sutra (*Prajnapa-
ramita*). The painting appears to be a northern view because the pagoda is
shown at the right. The rock with only two people sitting on it is most
likely the platform from which the monk [Chu] Tao-sheng (died A.D. 434)
expounded the Nirvāna Sutra (Li-p'an ching). Tao-sheng's original family
name was Wei. He was a student of the Mahāyāna teacher Kumārajīva
(died ca. 412) and translator of part of the Nirvāna Sutra.
      The history of this famous pilgrimage site includes the legend that
when Tao-sheng spoke, the audience did not believe, yet the rocks "nodded"
as if in agreement. *Chüeh-shih,* a phrase describing this event, was carved
into one of the rocks between the pagoda and the teaching platform. The
pavilion in the background is also part of the history of Tiger Hill.

Published: This painting was previously entitled "Rocky Ledges," then
"The Nodding Stone Terrace." Bibl. 19, p. 150; Bibl. 20, pp. 473–76, pl. 6,
fig. 8; Bibl. 22, p. 143, no. 52; Bibl. 25, pp. 4–7, fig. 6; Bibl. 33, vol. VII,
p. 229.

28. Old Pine Tree (Ch'iu-jan t'u)

Wen Cheng-ming (1470–1559), t. Cheng-chung, h. Heng-shan, original name Pi; from Su-chou, Chiangsu Province

Handscroll, ink on paper; H. 10 3/4 in. (27.3 cm.), L. 54 5/8 in. (138.8 cm.)

Purchase, Andrew R. and Martha Holden Jennings Fund 64.43   ill. p. 74

The two-line poem at the left end of the painting, signed by the artist, reads:

> Constantly its form is changing; chances are it never could
> be caught;
> Its dragon-whiskers bristle like lances, rank after rank.
> [signed] Cheng-ming.
>
>   (trans. Wai-kam Ho)

Following his signature are two seals of the artist (Wen Cheng-ming yin; Heng-shan).

Published: Bibl. 9, p. 225, ill. 811; Bibl. 10, p. 23a; Bibl. 25, pp. 7–8, fig. 2; Bibl. 33, vol. VII, p. 263 (listed under the title "A Branch of an old Juniper-tree").

29. Chrysanthemums (Mo-chü), 1490

T'ao Ch'eng (act. 1480–1532), t. Meng (or Mou)-hsüeh, h. Yün-hu hsien-jen; from Pao-ying, Chiangsu Province

Section of a handscroll, ink on paper; H. 11 1/4 in. (28.6 cm.), L. 59 7/8 in. (151.7 cm.)

Anonymous gift 60.40

The painting bears one seal of the artist (Yün-hu).

This is the first portion of a handscroll that consists of two individual paintings mounted together as one scroll. The second painting (not illustrated), which is in color, is entitled *Cabbages*, and the scroll in its entirety is called *Chrysanthemums and Cabbages* (Chü-shu t'u).

Published: Bibl. 30, cat. no. 43, pp. 76–77 (ill.); Bibl. 33, vol. IV, p. 221; Bibl. 33, vol. VII, p. 241; Bibl. 34, no. 19.

30. Ink Prunus (Mo-mei)

P'eng Hsü (act. ca. 1488–1521), t. Te-mien, h. Shih-chu; from K'un-shan, Chiangsu Province

Hanging scroll, ink on silk; H. 50 in. (127 cm.), W. 26 1/2 in. (67.3 cm.)

John L. Severance Fund 70.80

At the left middle edge of the painting are two seals of the artist.

Written sources indicate that P'eng Hsü had an impressive stylistic genealogy. He was the nephew of Chou Hao and continued his uncle's style of ink-prunus painting. Chou Hao (second half of the fifteenth century) was one of the followers of Wang Mien (1287–1366), the most important early Ming master of ink-prunus painting in the tradition of the Southern Sung master Yang Pu-chih (1097–1169); see No. 20.

Published: *CMAB* (February 1971), p. 50, ill. 128 (artist incorrectly listed as P'an Yü).

31. Taoist Retreat in Mountain and Stream, Landscape after Ni Tsan (Hsi-shan hsien-kuan t'u), 1567

Lu Chih (1496–1576), t. Shu-p'ing, h. Pao-shan; from Su-chou, Chiangsu Province

Hanging scroll, ink on paper; H. 42 15/16 in. (107.8 cm.), W. 18 in. (45.8 cm.)

Purchase, J. H. Wade Fund 62.43

The artist's inscription at the top of the painting reads:

In my youthful days I liked to imitate the ink method of Yün-lin [Ni Tsan]. Mr. Wen, the academician [Wen Cheng-ming] remarked that I barely succeeded in achieving some resemblance. He once honored me with the inscription "lofty and imperturbable indeed was the personality of Ni Yü [Ni, the Odd]. Pale ink and blue smoke were formed by his scribbling brush. His surviving works have become so rare in the last two hundred years; only Pao-shan [Lu Chih] carries on his true tradition." In my older years, having to comply with frequent requests for paintings, my brushwork has become stronger than before and I thought to myself that I may have surpassed the Old Master. In the year ting-mao *of Lung-ch'ing [1567] a friend brought a small painting [by Ni Tsan] and showed it to me in the mountains. I studied and enjoyed it for a long time, then realized that I was actually inferior. This gave me second thoughts about my earlier style so I picked up a piece of old window cloth and I had a piece of paper mounted on it. I did the painting in imitation. My friend was kind enough to say that it was truly a quick and close resemblance. I then wrote a colophon and presented the painting to him. My poem says:*

> "High mountains and distant waters are the thoughts coming from
> the lute;
> The drunken leaves and the sparse woods are merely flowers in the
> mirror.
> This idea, I'm sure, will be understood by Tzu-ch'i, one who appreciates
> my art,
> It is for him that I have painted on thin paper with light touches,
> The cloudy color of an autumn evening."

This is in the winter solstice of the same year. By then, Pao-shan, Mr. Lu, was already over seventy years of age. Could it be that one's brush also gets old together with one's age, as the saying goes. I put down my brush with a laugh.   (trans. Wai-kam Ho)

Following this inscription are two seals of the artist (Lu Shu-p'ing shih; Pao-shan-tzu); at the bottom left corner is another seal (Lu Chih ssu-yin).

The Ni Tsan painting from which this may have been "copied" is illustrated in *Chinese Paintings from the Chiang Er-shih Collection*, no. 12, an auction catalogue of Parke-Bernet Galleries, Inc., New York (March 5, 1971). Ni Tsan (1301–1374) was one of the Four Great Masters of the Yüan dynasty. His reputation was based on his sparse use of "dry ink."

Published: Bibl. 33, vol. VII, p. 214; Bibl. 42, no. 20 (ill.).

32. Mountains on a Clear Autumn Day (Chiang-shan ch'iu-ch'i)

Tung Ch'i-ch'ang (1555–1636), t. Hsüan-tsai, h. Ssu-weng; from Hua-t'ing (Sung-chiang), Chiangsu Province

Handscroll, ink on paper; H. 15 1/8 in. (38.4 cm.), L. 53 7/8 in. (136.8 cm.)

Purchase, J. H. Wade Fund 59.46

The artist's inscription at the left, following the painting, reads: "Huang Tzu-chiu's [Huang Kung-wang] *Mountains on a Clear Autumn Day* is like this. It is indeed regrettable that the Old Masters cannot see mine. [signed] Ssu-weng" (trans. Wai-kam Ho).

Huang Kung-wang (1269–1354) was perhaps the greatest of the Four Masters of the Yüan dynasty.

The Korean paper on which this painting was executed was presented to the throne of the Ming Emperor Wan-li (Shen-tsung, r. 1572–1620) from the Korean Imperial House. The writing of the tribute is recorded on the surface of the paper with very light gray characters; upon close scrutiny, much of the text can still be seen (though it is not visible in the catalogue ill.). This buff or cream-colored paper is known for its stiff, smooth surface.

Published: Bibl. 3, p. 19, ill. p. 18; Bibl. 7, p. 16, pl. 15; Bibl. 23, pp. 86–87, fig. 66; Bibl. 27, p. 50, ill. 8; Bibl. 30, cat. no. 64, pp. 112–113; Bibl. 44, pl. V; Bibl. 45, pl. I; Wen Fong, "The Orthodox Master," *The Academy: Art News Annual* 33 (New York, 1968), p. 135 (ill.).

33. Thin Forest and Distant Mountains (*Shu-lin yüan-shan*), 1628

Li Liu-fang (1575–1629), *t.* Ch'ang-heng, *h.* T'an-yüan; from Hsi-hsien, Anhui Province, moved to Chia-ting, Chiangsu Province
Hanging scroll, ink on paper; H. 45 in. (114.3 cm.), W. 15 7/8 in. (39.7 cm.)
John L. Severance Fund 53.630

The artist's inscription at the top of the painting reads:

> *Thin forest and distant mountains have always attracted me;*
> *As if they were from the brush and ink of Ni Tsan, left behind*
>   *by the master in this mortal world.*
> *Now that the quiet recluse has chosen to live in the South of*
>   *the City,*
> *He paints the spring breeze—over a curve of the river.*
>
> *In the spring day of* wu-ch'en [1628] *I made this painting*
> *and attached an old poem.* [signed] *Li Liu-fang.* [Bibl. 22]

Following the signature are two seals of the artist (Li Liu-fang-yin; Chang-heng shih).

Published: Bibl. 12, figs. 68, 69; Bibl. 13, p. 674; Bibl. 19, p. 96, ill. 71; Bibl. 22, p. 88, ill. 68; Bibl. 23, p. 438, fig. 582; Bibl. 30, cat. no. 71, pp. 126–127 (ill.); Bibl. 33, vol. VII, p. 208; Bibl. 38, vol. II, p. 360.

34. Conversation with a Priest (*Chih-Hsü ch'ing-yen t'u*), 1643

Lan Ying (1585–1664), *t.* T'ien-shu, *h.* Tieh-sou; from Ch'ien-t'ang (Hang-chou), Chechiang Province
Hanging scroll, ink on paper; H. 55 7/16 in. (140.8 cm.), W. 22 in. (55.9 cm.)
Gift of Stephen O. K. Chen 70.128

In his inscription at the top of the painting, Lan Ying writes that he painted this for his friend, the Ch'an teacher Wu-yün, whom he compared to the famous Six Dynasties monk Chih-tun (died ca. 366). Thus the two figures portrayed here, engrossed in their "pure conversation," are Lan Ying himself and Wu-yün, who is facing outward. The inscription is followed by two seals of the artist (Lan ying chih-yin; T'ien-shu fu).

35. Meditative Visit to a Mountain Retreat (*Yen-hsi ssu-fang*), 1648

Hsiang Sheng-mo (1597–1658), *t.* K'ung-chang, *h.* Hsü-shan-jen; from Chia-hsing, Chechiang Province
Handscroll, ink on paper; H. 12 in. (30.5 cm.), L. 107 1/2 in. (273 cm.)
Purchase, J. H. Wade Fund 62.42

The painting bears a signed inscription dated *wu-tzu* (1648), as well as nine seals of the artist: T'ien-lai-ko-chung-wen-sun; Hsiang-shih-k'ung-chang-tsui-hsin-han-mo; Ch'ing-fu-yüan-chung-ti-i-mao-yeh; (2) T'u-wu-so; K'ao-ku-cheng-chin; Wei-ch'ang-pieh-chü-shou-yen; Hsiang K'ung-chang shih; Wei-sang-ssu-wen.

36. The Mountains of the Five Cataracts (*Wu-hsieh-shan*)

Ch'en Hung-shou (1598–1652), *t.* Chang-hou, *h.* Lao-lien; from Chu-chi, Chechiang Province
Hanging scroll, ink on silk; H. 46 9/16 in. (118.2 cm.), W. 20 15/16 in. (53.2 cm.)
John L. Severance Fund 66.366

The artist's signature (Hung-shou) and one seal (Ch'en) are placed by the lower right corner of the painting.

This may well be an early work by Ch'en, for it is said that in his youth he traveled with some older friends to this spot, which was near his home in Chechiang Province (see Appendix). The style and the unpretentious qualities of the painting, such as the signature with no inscription and the anonymous solitary man, suggest that it might have been done in commemoration of that journey.

Published: Bibl. 10, 299b; Bibl. 27, p. 57, no. 28; Bibl. 33, vol. VI, pl. 315; Bibl. 38, vol. II, pl. 376; James Cahill, *The Restless Landscape: Chinese Painting of the Late Ming Period* (Berkeley, 1971), cat. no. 69 (ill.).

37. Clouds Visiting a Mountain Retreat (*Fang Kao Shang-shu yün-shan t'u*), 1633

T'ao Hung (act. ca. 1610–1640), *t.* Ch'iu-shui, *h.* Yen-shan; from Hunan Province, moved to Nan-ching, Chiangsu Province, and Yünnan Province
Hanging scroll, ink on paper; H. 69 1/2 in. (176.4 cm.), W. 39 3/4 in. (100.3 cm.)
Andrew R. and Martha Holden Jennings Fund 71.19

The artist's inscription reads: "Imitating Kao Fang-shan's [Kao K'o-kung, ca. 1245–ca. 1310] brush at Liu-yün-ho [Valley of Lingering Clouds] during a spring day in *kuei-yu* [1633]. [signed] Yen-shan, T'ao Hung." Following this are two seals of the artist (T'ao Hung chih-yin; Tzu-ch'iu-shui).

Until recently, very little was known about the early life of T'ao Hung. Research by Wai-kam Ho has established that T'ao Hung was a contemporary of Sheng Mao-yeh (act. ca. 1607–1637), and their works were stylistically similar. T'ao Hung moved his family to Nan-ching, Chiangsu Province, and settled there in his old age. His son became a friend of Kung Hsien (see Nos. 39, 40), famous leader of the "Nanking School," and this relationship perhaps explains the stylistic kinship between T'ao Hung and the younger master. In 1644, after the collapse of the Ming dynasty, T'ao Hung joined the last group of loyalist resisters in Yünnan Province. In 1645, when the resistance was finally crushed by the Manchu, he fled to Burma, where he died not long after. Only four other works by T'ao Hung are known today, and they are all in private collections.

Published: Bibl. 28, p. 322, ills. 68, 69.

38. Landscape in the Style of Wu Chen (*Fang Mei-tao-jen pi-i*), 1668

Hsiao Yün-ts'ung (1596–1673), *t.* Ch'ih-mu, *h.* Wu-men tao-jen; from Wu-hu, Anhui Province
Album leaf, ink on paper; H. 8 1/4 in. (20.9 cm.), W. 6 3/16 in. (15.7 cm.)
John L. Severance Fund 55.302a   *ill. p. 89*

The artist's poem at the upper right reads:

> *I love Mei Tao-jen* [*Wu Chen*]
> *Whose brushes often have strange thoughts;*
> *Between the heavy modeling and deep coloring,*
> *One finds himself, as it were, in real forest and wilderness.*
>   [signed] *Yün-ts'ung.*
>
>   (trans. Wen Fong)

One seal of the artist (Hsiao Yün-ts'ung) follows the signature.
This is the second leaf of an eight-leaf album of various seasonal landscapes (*Ch'iu-feng hsiao-se t'u*). The last leaf is dated to the tenth month of *wu-shen* (1668).

Published: *CMAB* (June 1957), p. 124, ill. 2.

39. Marshy Landscape (*Sui-kuo ch'un-k'ung*)
Kung Hsien (ca. 1620–1689), *t.* Pan-ch'ien, *h.* Yeh-i; from K'un-shan;
lived in Nan-ching, Chiangsu Province
Album leaf, ink on paper; H. 12 1/2 in. (31.8 cm.), W. 18 in. (45.7 cm.)
Andrew R. and Martha Holden Jennings Fund 70.19   *ill. p. 94*

One seal of the artist (Pan-ch'ien) is near the left edge of the painting.

Published: Bibl. 28, p. 322, ill. 67; Bibl. 30, cat. no. 125, pp. 214–15
(ill.); Bibl. 37, p. 151, ill. 9.

40. Landscape in the Style of Tung Yüan and Chü-jan (*Fang Tung-*
Chü pi-i), 1650
Kung Hsien (ca. 1620–1689), *t.* Pan-ch'ien, *h.* Yeh-i; from K'un-shan;
lived in Nan-ching, Chiangsu Province
Hanging scroll, ink on silk; H. 85 3/16 in (216.3 cm.), W. 22 5/8 in.
(57.5 cm.)
Andrew R. and Martha Holden Jennings Fund 69.123

The painting bears an inscription dated *keng-hsü* (1670), followed by
two seals of the artist (Kung Pan-ch'ien; Yeh-i Hsien).

Kung Hsien states in his inscription that he had painted this picture
twenty years earlier (1650). He then explains that Wu Chin-ming, the
owner of the work, met him in Nan-ching, where they discussed painting,
and Kung Hsien added his inscription at that time.

Published: Bibl. 28, p. 322, ill. 66; James Cahill, "The Early Style of Kung
Hsien," *Oriental Art*, vol. XVI, no. 1 (Spring 1970), p. 60, fig. 17.

41. Landscape after Mi Fei (*Fang Mi-lao pi-i*), 1684
Ch'a Shih-piao (1615–1698), *t.* Erh-chan, *h.* Mei-ho, from Hsiu-ning,
Anhui Province
Album leaf, ink on paper; H. 9 7/16 in. (23.9 cm.), W. 12 3/4 in. (32.4 cm.)
Mr. and Mrs. Severance A. Millikin Collection 55.37i

The artist's inscription at the top of the painting reads: "Pei-yüan's
[Tung Yüan] painting of receding mountain peaks is wholesome and rich.
None but the Elder Mi [Mi Fei] was capable of it. [signed] Erh-chan"
(trans. Wen Fong).

Over the inscription is one seal of the artist (Shih-piao); another is
at the bottom left corner.

This painting and No. 42 are from a twelve-leaf landscape album in
various styles entitled *Wu-ling ch'i-ching*. It is dated *chia-tzu* (1684) on
three of the leaves. Mi Fei or Fu (1052–1107) was the greatest exponent of
the "wet-ink" style.

Published: Bibl. 27, p. 54, ill. 24; Bibl. 33, vol. VII, p. 284.

42. Yangtze River Scenery after Huang Kung-wang (*Fang Ta-ch'ih*
ch'ang-chiang sheng-lan t'u), 1684
Ch'a Shih-piao (1615–1698), *t.* Erh-chan, *h.* Mei-ho; from Hsiu-ning,
Anhui Province
Album leaf, ink on paper; H. 9 7/16 in. (23.9 cm.), W. 12 3/4 in. (32.4 cm.)
Mr. and Mrs. Severance A. Millikin Collection 55.37f

The artist's inscription at the top of the painting reads: "After the
idea of the *Yangtze River Scenery* by Ta-ch'ih [Huang Kung-wang]. Shih-
piao, while visiting the Tai-yen-lou [Tower of Waiting for the Wild Geese]
at Yang-chou" (trans. Wai-kam Ho).

Over the inscription is one seal of the artist (Shih-piao); another (Erh-
chan) is at the bottom left corner.

This and the preceding leaf (No. 41) are from the landscape album
entitled *Wu-ling ch'i-ching*. According to the index of recorded Chinese
paintings (Bibl. 10), Huang Kung-wang's *Ch'ang-chiang sheng-lan t'u* is one
of the better paintings by this master of the Yüan dynasty.

The previous title of this painting was *Scenery of Mt. Ch'ang-pai after*
Huang Kung-wang (*Ta-ch'ih Ch'ang-pai sheng-lan t'u*). The fourth character of the inscribed title is not very clear, but from the other characters
as well as what is known about Huang Kung-wang's work, a reading of
"Ch'ang-chiang" (Yangtze River) is preferable. Ch'ang-pai (Mt. Everlast-
ing-White) is a mountain range on the China-Korea border that probably
neither Huang Kung-wang nor Ch'a Shih-piao visited.

Published: Bibl. 22, p. 150; Bibl. 27, p. 54, ill. 25 (incorrectly labeled
"Landscape after Ni Tsan"); Bibl. 33, vol. VII, p. 284.

43. Landscape in the Style of Shen Chou (*Fang Shih-t'ien pi-i*), 1690
Mei Ch'ing (1623–1697), *t.* Yüan-kung, *h.* Chü-chan; from Hsüan-ch'eng,
Anhui Province
Album leaf, ink on paper; H. 11 1/4 in. (28.6 cm.), W. 17 5/16 in. (44 cm.)
John L. Severance Fund 62.157c

The artist's signed inscription at the left of the painting is dated
summer, *keng-wu* (1690). There are also five seals of the artist (San-mei-yu;
Chü-hsing Ch'ing; Yüan-kung; Hua-sung; Po-chien-shan-k'ou-jen-chia).
This painting and No. 44 are from a ten-leaf landscape album by Mei
Ch'ing, one of the "four masters of Anhui."

Published: Bibl. 10, p. 285; Bibl. 19, p. 157; Bibl. 22, p. 150; Bibl. 30, cat.
no. 110, p. 190; Bibl. 35, ill. p. 95b.

44. Landscape in the Style of the Ching-Kuan School (*Fang Ching-*
Kuan pi-i), 1690
Mei Ch'ing (1623–1697), *t.* Yüan-kung, *h.* Chü-chan; from Hsüan-ch'eng,
Anhui Province
Album leaf, ink on paper; H. 11 1/4 in. (28.6 cm.), W. 17 5/16 in. (44 cm.)
John L. Severance Fund 62.157h

The painting bears a poem by the artist at the top left, as well as three
of his seals (Chü-hsing Ch'ing; Hua-sung; Chü-hsing Hsien-i). The third
leaf of the landscape album of which this painting and No. 43 are a part is
dated 1690. The "Ching-Kuan School" is a reference to Ching Hao and
Kuan T'ung (act. tenth to eleventh centuries), traditionally regarded as
the founders of monumental-style landscape painting.

Published: Bibl. 10, p. 285; Bibl. 19, p. 157; Bibl. 22, p. 150; Bibl. 30, cat.
no. 110, p. 190.

45. Fish and Rocks (*Yü-shih t'u*)
Chu Ta (1626–1705), *t.* Ta-wu, *h.* Pa-ta-shan-jen, original name T'ung-
hsin (?); from Nan-ch'ang, Chianghsi Province
Handscroll, ink on paper; H. 11 1/2 in. (29.2 cm.), L. 62 in. (157.4 cm.)
John L. Severance Fund 53.247

The artist's poem following the overhanging rock with chrysanthemums reads:

A foot and a half from heaven
Only white clouds are moving.
Are there yellow flowers there?
Behind the clouds is the city of gold.

The artist's poem above the two fish reads:

In the old days there was a river,
Above which the bright moon used to shine.
Mr. Huang had two golden carp
Which have gone, becoming dragons.

The artist's poem above the lotus reads:

Under these thirty-six thousand acres [of lotus]
Day and night fish are swimming.
Coming here to the shadow of a yellow cliff
All creatures become immortal.

(trans. Wen Fong)

There is an artist's seal at the beginning of the scroll and one seal (I-shan-jen) after each poem.

Chu Ta, who spent part of his life as a Buddhist monk, has been called an individualist, an eccentric, and a fantastic. According to legend, he became insane during the later part of his life. The wording and style of the signature on this painting suggest that it was done around 1694.

Published: Bibl. 4, pl. 27; Bibl. 12, figs. 30, 31; Bibl. 16, ill. p. 199; Bibl. 20, pp. 483–84, pl. 14, fig. 19; Bibl. 23, p. 451, fig. 593; Bibl. 27, p. 59, ill. 36; Bibl. 30, cat. no. 118, pp. 204–5 (ill.); Bibl. 33, vol. VI, pl. 384b; Bibl. 33, vol. VII, p. 325; Bibl. 35, p. 262, fig. d; Bibl. 36, p. 195, fig. 137; *CMAB* (November 1958), pp. 215–17 (ill.); Roger Goepper, *The Oriental World* (New York, 1967), pl. 84; Fred Fang-yu Wang, "The Album of Flower Studies Signed 'Ch'uan-Ch'i' in the Palace Museum and the Early Work of Chu Ta," *Proceedings of the International Symposium on Chinese Painting*, National Palace Museum, June 1970 (Taipei, 1972), pp. 543, 544, pl. 20; Vito Giacalone, *Chu Ta: A Selection of Painting and Calligraphy*, exhibition catalogue, Vassar College Art Gallery (Poughkeepsie, N.Y., 1972), cat. no. 8 (ill.).

46. Tall Bamboo and Distant Mountains after Wang Meng

(Lin Wang Meng Hsiu-chu yüan-shan), 1694
Wang Hui (1632–1717), *t.* Shih-ku, *h.* Keng-yen san-jen; from Ch'ang-shu, Chiangsu Province
Hanging scroll, ink on paper; H. 31 1/4 in. (79.3 cm.), W. 15 1/2 in. (39.5 cm.)
John L. Severance Fund 53.629

The artist's inscription, copied from Wang Meng's painting, reads:

"Previously, Wen Hu-chou [Wen T'ung] painted a scroll called A Horizontal View of the Evening Mist, *with an inscription by Emperor Kao-tsung [Ssu-ling] of the Sung dynasty later added on its beginning. The strength of its brush is not inferior to Kuo Hsi; and the bamboos between the trees and rocks are beyond the usual criteria of brush and ink since they are the direct overflow of the artist's feelings. Professor Tzu-wen has asked me for a painting of tall bamboo and distant mountains. It is a pity that my brush cannot be compared with Kuo [Hsi], nor is it anywhere near that of Hu-chou. These few scribbles of rough and clumsy brush can only be taken as an expression of a moment's interest painted for gratifying Kuang-wen's graciousness. —Huang-he-shan-chung-jen, Wang Meng."* Chia-hsü [1694], *ninth month, copied for I-weng at Ch'ang-an. [signed] Hai-yü Wang Hui.* [Bibl. 22]

Two seals of the artist follow his signature (Wang Hui chih-yin; Shih-ku-tzu).

Wen T'ung (1018–1079) and Kuo Hsi (ca. 1020–ca. 1075), mentioned in the inscription, were Northern Sung dynasty painters famous for their pictures of bamboo and landscapes, respectively. The painting of which this may be a "copy" is illustrated in the *Museum of Far Eastern Antiquities Bulletin*, no. 36 (Stockholm, 1964).

Published: Bibl. 14, pp. 103–4, fig. 84; Bibl. 22, p. 98, fig. 79; Bibl. 33, vol. VII, p. 427; Bibl. 36, p. 193, pl. 135; *Masterpieces of Chinese Painting: Collection of P'ang Shu [sic] Chai, Esq.* (Shanghai, 1940), vol. III, pl. 11.

47. Landscape with Waterfall *(Ch'i-yen Fei-p'u)*

Li Shih-cho (act. 1741–ca. 1765), *t.* Han-chang, *h.* Ch'ing-chai-chü-shih; from San-han, Korea-Manchuria
Hanging scroll, ink on paper; H. 35 7/8 in. (91.1 cm.), W. 16 1/8 in. (41.3 cm.)
John L. Severance Fund 52.588

The artist's inscription at the top right reads:

Ching Hao called himself Hung-ku-tzu and wrote an essay titled Shan-shui-chüeh. *He had once boastfully criticized that Wu Tao-tzu has brush but no ink, and Hsiang Yung [T'ang dynasty] has ink but no brush. Therefore, Hung-ku [Ching Hao] has mastered both ink and brush, and later Kuan T'ung followed him. They are the best of the T'ang and Sung masters. I am here imitating the merits of Ching Hao, and have discarded his weakness. [signed] Li Shih-cho.* [Bibl. 22]

The painting also bears four seals of the artist (Cho-shih; Ku-chai; Fan-yen-ching-yen-chien-hsing-ch'ing; Yüan-chan-shang).

Published: Bibl. 19, p. 139, fig. 114; Bibl. 20, pl. 12, fig. 16; Bibl. 22, p. 132, fig. 105; Bibl. 33, vol. VI, pl. 442; Bibl. 33, vol. VII, p. 376.

Plates: Ceramics

48. Ovoid Jar. Early T'ang dynasty. Buff
stoneware. H. 10 7/8 in. (27.6 cm.)

49. Phoenix-head Ewer. Early Northern
Sung dynasty. Ch'ing-pai ware, porcelain.
H. 15 1/4 in. (38.7 cm.)

51. Baluster Vase with Peony Design.
Early Northern Sung dynasty. Tz'u-chou
ware, stoneware. H. 16 3/8 in. (41.6 cm.)

50. Ewer. Early Northern Sung dynasty.
Tz'u-chou ware, buff-gray stoneware.
H. 6 7/8 in. (17.5 cm.)

52. Pillow. Northern Sung dynasty. Tz'u-chou ware, buff stoneware. H. 4 5/8 in. (11.8 cm.), L. 17 3/8 in. (44.1 cm.), W. 7 3/4 in. (19.8 cm.). Opposite above

53. Jar. Northern Sung dynasty. Tz'u-chou ware, gray stoneware. H. 4 1/2 in. (11.4 cm.). Opposite below

56. Covered Box. Northern Sung dynasty. Ting ware, white-gray porcelain. H. (with cover) 1 5/8 in. (4.1 cm.), Diam. 4 1/8 in. (10.5 cm.)

55. Jar. Northern Sung dynasty. Tz'u-chou ware, buff stoneware. H. 4 3/8 in. (11.1 cm.)

60. Conical Bowl. Chin dynasty. Ting ware, grayish white porcelain. H. 2 1/2 in. (6.5 cm.), Diam. 8 1/4 in. (21 cm.)

59. Bowl. Chin dynasty. Ting ware, grayish white porcelain. H. 3 3/8 in. (8.6 cm.), Diam. 10 1/4 in. (26 cm.). Lower left

57. Conical Bowl. Northern Sung dynasty. Ting ware, grayish white porcelain. H. 2 1/2 in. (6.4 cm.), Diam. 8 in. (20.3 cm.). Lower right

58. Basin. Northern Sung dynasty. Ting ware, light gray porcelain. H. 6 1/4 in. (15.9 cm.), Diam. 12 in. (30.5 cm.). Opposite above

61. Bowl. Yüan dynasty. Shu-fu ware, creamy-paste porcelain. H. 3 1/8 in. (7.9 cm.), Diam. 6 3/4 in. (17.2 cm.). Opposite below

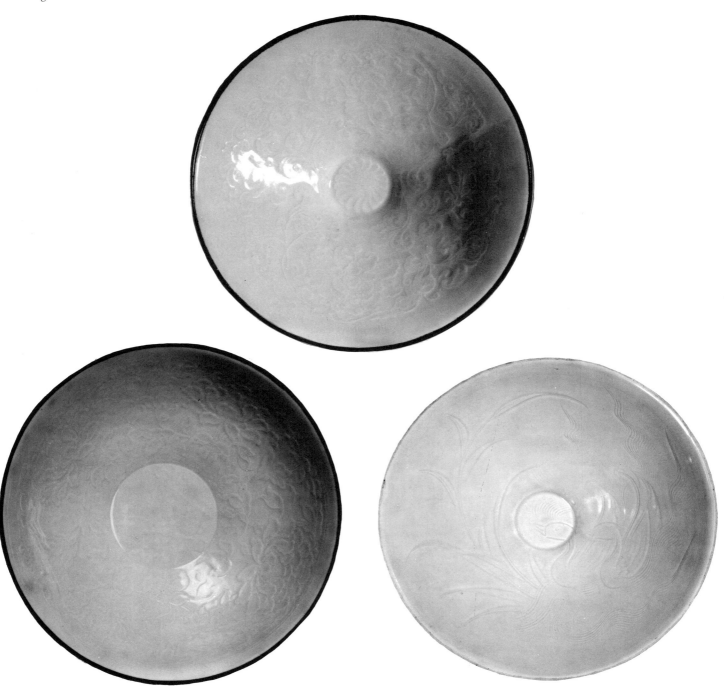

62. Wine Jar. Yüan dynasty. Tz'u-chou ware, stoneware. H. 12 1/2 in. (31.8 cm.)

63. Jar. Yüan dynasty. Tz'u-chou ware, buff-gray stoneware. H. 11 in. (27.9 cm.). Opposite

64. Potter with Double-gourd Vase.
Yüan dynasty. Ch'ing-pai ware, porcelain.
H. 5 1/8 in. (13.1 cm.)

65. Chüeh. Ming dynasty. White porcelain.
H. 6 in. (15.3 cm.)

66. Mei-p'ing Vase. Ming dynasty. White
porcelain. H. 12 5/8 in. (32.1 cm.). Opposite

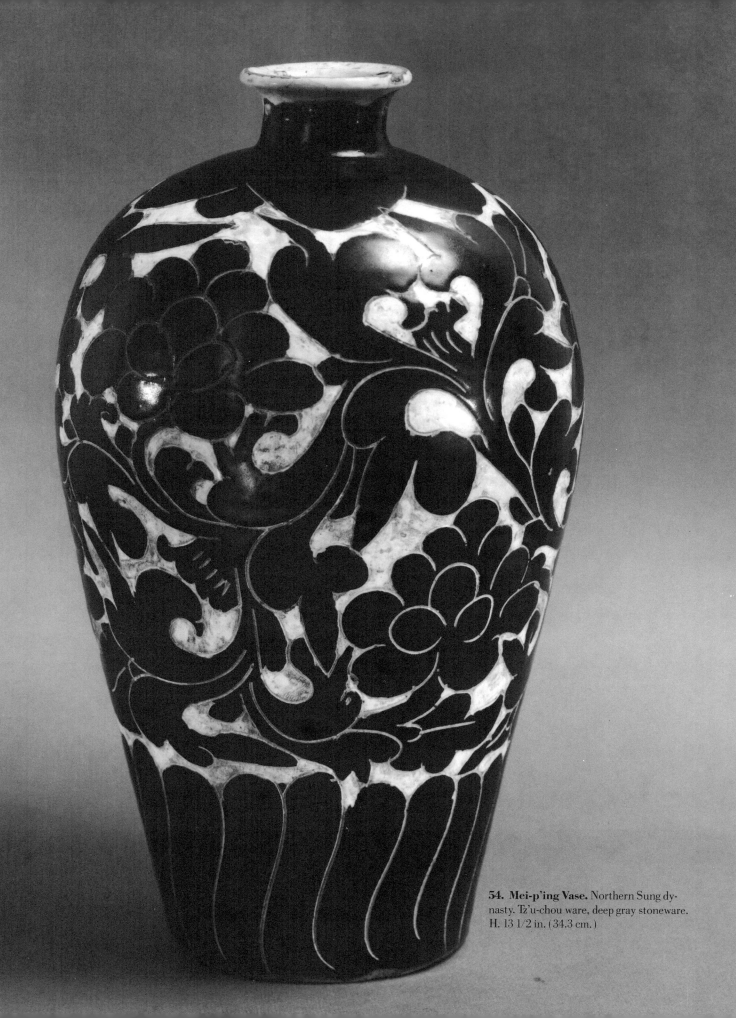

54. Mei-p'ing Vase. Northern Sung dynasty. Tz'u-chou ware, deep gray stoneware. H. 13 1/2 in. (34.3 cm.)

Catalogue: Ceramics

48. Ovoid Jar
Early T'ang dynasty
Buff stoneware; H. 10 7/8 in. (27.6 cm.)
Charles W. Harkness Endowment Fund 30.323

Four loop handles are placed on the shoulder at the base of a short, straight neck. Both inside and out the jar is covered with a cream-white slip, over which is a crackled transparent glaze that stops above the short, slightly flaring base. The base is very slightly concave. On the shoulder a lightly incised line encircles the jar, passing through the loop handles.

The proportions and style of the jar and handles are those of the early T'ang dynasty (seventh century); see *Wen Wu*, no. 3, 1972, pp. 34–48 (note type 5, chart 3). Recent discoveries in China suggest a provenance in Honan Province.

Published: Bibl. 41, cat. no. 91, ill. p. 65; *CMAB* (November 1931), pp. 174–75, ill. p. 183; Michael Sullivan, *Chinese Ceramics, Bronzes and Jades in the Collection of Sir Alan and Lady Barlow* (London, 1963), p. 35.

49. Phoenix-head Ewer
Early Northern Sung dynasty
Ch'ing-pai ware, porcelain; H. 15 1/4 in. (38.7 cm.)
Mr. and Mrs. Severance A. Millikin Collection 65.468

The head has been reliably restored on the original remains and has been reattached to the tapered neck, which is marked by two sharp ridges. There are three incised lines on the shoulder. The melon-shaped body has seven lobes. The pale green-white glaze is slightly worn in some areas; has several iron imperfections (brown-black spots) of varying sizes; and is absent on the bottom within the slightly flaring foot, the rim of which has remnants of sandy spur marks.

This ewer has been classified by Wirgin as "Cp 36," Five Dynasties–Northern Sung dynasty (Bibl. 46).*

Published: Bibl. 1, vol. XX, p. 86, fig. 6; Bibl. 46, p. 67, pl. 29i; *CMAB* (September 1966), ill. p. 268.

50. Ewer
Early Northern Sung dynasty
Tz'u-chou ware, buff-gray stoneware; H. 6 7/8 in. (17.5 cm.)
Purchase, J. H. Wade Fund 48.219

The cream-white slip covering all but the interior was carved to create a bold floral scroll. The shoulder band has two layers, each of six petals. The central design alternates above and below a winding stem; its major components are two leaves, which flank a stylized flower placed

*The classification of Sung wares adopted here is that of J. Wirgin (Bibl. 46); i.e., "Cp" means Ch'ing-pai; "Tc," Tz'u-chou; "Ti," Ting. The numbers refer to the shapes and decorations distinguished by Wirgin and numbered by him.

below the spout. Although it is of the same period as the body, the spout appears to be an addition. A transparent glaze covers all but the foot (and the interior), giving a "wet" look to the natural stoneware, the background for the design. The handle is ear-shaped.

This ewer has been classified as type "Tc 1" and compared with Teng-feng (Honan) fragments, though it is traditionally labeled Hsiu-wu (Honan) ware (Bibl. 46).

Published: Bibl. 14, pl. 6; Bibl. 23, p. 363, fig. 473; Bibl. 31, p. 213; Bibl. 41, cat. no. 230, p. 90; Bibl. 46, pl. 41b; Henri Rivière, *La Céramique dans l'art d'Extrême-Orient* (Paris, 1923), p. 213, pl. 58; *CMAB* (January 1949), pp. 13–14, ill. p. 11; "Far Eastern Art," *Far Eastern Quarterly*, vol. IX, no. 1 (November 1949), p. 69; *Tōsetsu*, no. 41 (August 1956), ill. p. 46.

51. Baluster Vase with Peony Design
Early Northern Sung dynasty
Tz'u-chou ware, stoneware; H. 16 3/8 in. (41.5 cm.)
Purchase, J. H. Wade Fund 48.226

The shoulder design of feathery leaves, the wide central band of four stylized peony flowers alternating above and below their thin, scroll-like stem, and the lower band of a formal palmette scroll were most likely effected by lightly incising the design onto the plain body, then covering the entire design with a thin, cream-white slip, and finally wiping off the white—thus leaving it embedded in the incisions. The natural color of the body (slightly darkened by the glaze) appears as the background. A cream-white slip was also applied to the neck and lower body, and a clear glaze over all. The inside of the flaring foot was left unglazed. In the middle of one side are three scars resulting from contact with something during the firing.

Wares of this type have been known as Hsiu-wu, Tang-yang-yü, and Chiao-tso wares (all of Honan Province). Following recent excavations in Teng-feng hsien (Honan Province), this was classified by Wirgin (Bibl. 46) as type "Tc 2" from that locale. The shape is very characteristic of the Liao and early Sung dynasties.

Published: Bibl. 14, pl. 31; Bibl. 15, fig. 22, p. 213; Bibl. 18, pl. IV; Bibl. 23, p. 364, fig. 475; Bibl. 31, ill. p. 213; Bibl. 41, p. 90, fig. 228; Bibl. 46, pl. 40i; *CMAB* (January 1949), pp. 13–14, ill. p. 10; *Far Eastern Quarterly*, vol. IX, no. 1 (1949), p. 69; Junkichi Mayuyama, *Chinese Ceramics in the West* (Tokyo, 1960), pl. 36; Jakuji Hasabe and Seizo Hayashiya, eds., *Chugoku kotoji* [Chinese Ceramics], vol. I, pt. 1, ill. 152.

52. Pillow
Northern Sung dynasty
Tz'u-chou ware, buff stoneware; H. 4 5/8 in. (11.8 cm.), L. 17 3/8 in. (44.1 cm.), W. 7 3/4 in. (19.8 cm.)
Edward L. Whittemore Fund 40.50

The white slip, covering all but the flat bottom, was carved away to create a three-panel design on the top surface of the pillow. (The central design is worthy of comparison with the Ming dynasty painting by Pien Wen-chin, No. 25.) Brown slip was applied to all the excised spaces, except for the corners of the central rectangular panel where the natural body is revealed. A transparent glaze was applied over all but the bottom. There is a hole in the right, front, vertical panel which allowed air to escape during the firing and cooling process.

This pillow has been classified as "Tc 19" and correlated to types from Fen-chou (Shanhsi Province); it has characteristics in common with examples from Hopei (Bibl. 46).

Published: Bibl. 14, pl. 45; Bibl. 31, ill. p. 212; Bibl. 46, pl. 48e; *CMAB* (October 1941), pp. 125–26, ill. p. 131.

53. Jar
Northern Sung dynasty
Tz'u-chou ware, gray stoneware; H. 4 1/2 in. (11.4 cm.)
Gift of Dr. and Mrs. Sherman E. Lee 64.500

A white slip was applied to this oblate jar, covering the entire area from inside the neck, over the body, to just above the slightly flaring foot. It was carved away to create six stylized leaves, alternating above and below their curving stem. A transparent glaze covers all but the lowest area. One side of the jar has three long crazes. The underside of the foot shows ochre discolorations. Within the foot is an unclear ink inscription, which may read "Lo-erh Residence" (Lo-erh fu).

54. Mei-p'ing Vase
Northern Sung dynasty
Tz'u-chou ware, deep gray stoneware; H. 13 1/2 in. (34.3 cm.)
Purchase, J. H. Wade Fund 40.52

Black slip, applied over the white slip which extends to just inside the mouth, was carved away to create a band of overlapping lotus petals around the collar, a central design of six peonies, as well as ten stylized leaves around the base. A thin white slip was brushed onto the body afterward, filling the spaces within the central design. The bottom is flat except for a circular, gouged groove.

The base has been classified as "Tc 23," a style that continued well into the Chin dynasty (Bibl. 46).

Published: Bibl. 31, ill. p. 213; Bibl. 41, p. 92, fig. 236; Bibl. 46, p. 106; *CMAB* (November 1940), pp. 142–43, ill. p. 130.

55. Jar
Northern Sung dynasty
Tz'u-chou ware, buff stoneware; H. 4 3/8 in. (11.1 cm.)
Gift of Dr. and Mrs. Sherman E. Lee 64.501

Two small handles reach from the middle of the short neck to the shoulders. A black-brown slip covers all but the lower portion of the body, the slightly flaring foot, and a ring around the middle of the interior. Raised, vertical ribs of white slip are placed at regular intervals in six groups around the body (4, 2, 3, 3, 3, 3). A thick, transparent glaze covers all of the outside slip and unevenly covers the top quarter of the interior.

This ware, once called Honan Temmoku ware, has been classified as "Tc 32," with provenances of Honan and Hopei (Bibl. 46).

Published: Bibl. 41, cat. no. 250 (ill.); Bibl. 46, p. 116.

56. Covered Box
Northern Sung dynasty
Ting ware, white-gray porcelain; H. (with cover) 1 5/8 in. (4.1 cm.),

Diam. 4 1/8 in. (10 cm.)
John L. Severance Fund 57.32

The cover is incised with a design of a large lotus leaf, seen from the side, and lotus flowers with pointed petals. The sides of the cover and of the lower half are encircled by incised lines. There are unglazed scratches on the sloping lower part of the box and within the foot. A grayish glaze covers all but the beveled foot, its rim, a ring on the inside center bottom, and the contiguous surfaces of the cover and box.

57. Conical Bowl
Northern Sung dynasty
Ting ware, grayish white porcelain; H. 2 1/2 in. (6.4 cm.), Diam. 8 in. (20.3 cm.)
Dudley P. Allen Fund 29.995

Within a thin, incised circle, two ducks (symbolic of conjugal fidelity) float side by side on combed waves before reeds. A thick, ivory glaze covers all but the lip, upon which the bowl rested during the firing. Near the foot are some small areas of exposed body. One area bears "tear-marks." Such marks (*lei hen*), which have been considered the indication of true Ting ware, are spots where the glaze has coagulated and streaked with a resulting deeper coloring.

A bowl with copper-bound rim, virtually identical with this, has been classified as "Ti 18," and another with the rim bound in copper has been dated as eleventh–twelfth century (Bibl. 29).

Published: *CMAB* (March 1930), pp. 42, 43, ill. p. 47.

58. Basin
Northern Sung dynasty
Ting ware, light gray porcelain; H. 6 1/4 in. (15.9 cm.), Diam. 12 in. (30.5 cm.)
Fanny Tewksbury King Collection 56.702

The slightly flaring lip of this large basin has two grooves. The exterior is decorated with four rows of overlapping lotus petals in low relief. A freely incised and combed lotus flower, leaf, and stem appear on the inside, below an incised circular line. On the inside there are several black dots, glaze imperfections, and on the bottom two small scrapes expose the body. The bowl's curvature continues within the foot rim. The top rim is unglazed and the foot is glazed, which shows that this basin was fired on its mouth rim. There are tear-marks on a section of the exterior.

The most probable kiln sites for Ting ware are Chien-tz'u Ts'un and Yen-shan Ts'un, both about sixteen miles north of Ch'ü-yang, Hopei Province. Bibl. 29 contains a good explanation of the historical and geographical provenance of Ting ware.

59. Bowl
Chin dynasty
Ting ware, grayish white porcelain; H. 3 3/8 in. (8.6 cm.), Diam. 10 1/4 in. (26 cm.)
John L. Severance Fund 57.49

The molded design consists of four large peonies surrounded by buds and leaves. On the exterior an incised (accidental?) line, near the bottom, almost encircles the body. On the inside of the foot are regular, closely spaced, oblique impressions. Several small areas, notably parts of the foot rim, are devoid of glaze and appear tan owing to high firing. Since the bowl rested on the mouth rim during the firing, the rim is unglazed and has been fitted with a soldered copper (or copper alloy) band, which has tarnished over the years.

Published: Bibl. 23, p. 365, fig. 478.

60. Conical Bowl

Chin dynasty
Ting ware, grayish white porcelain; H. 2 1/2 in. (6.5 cm.), Diam. 8 1/4 in. (21 cm.)
Fanny Tewksbury King Collection 56.699

The molded peony design (with four main flowers) is surrounded by a rectangular key-fret pattern at the lip. A stylized, nineteen-petal flower is at the center. The mouth has a tarnished copper rim which has been joined and soldered. In addition to tear-marks there are two sections of *ku-ch'u* ("exposed bones" or bare patches without glaze) on the exterior.

This bowl has been classified as "Ti 36" (Bibl. 46).

Published: Bibl. 46, p. 146.

61. Bowl

Yüan dynasty
Shu-fu ware, creamy-paste porcelain; H. 3 1/8 in. (7.9 cm.), Diam. 6 3/4 in. (17.2 cm.)
Anonymous gift 53.122

The design consists of three staggered bands of fluting (forty-six stylized petals form each band); two characters—*Fu* (good fortune) and *Lu* (governmental and material success), which previously were read incorrectly as *Shou* (longevity) and *Fu* (good fortune); and a dotted spiral within a ring at the bottom center. The thick-rimmed, unglazed foot and spots of exposed body and lip rim are burned to a light salmon-tan color. Within one flute is a disc of turquoise imperfection in an otherwise smooth, light bluish-gray, milky glaze.

The usual inscription from which the ware derives its name are the characters *Shu* and *Fu*, meaning palace use. Shu-fu ware is generally considered to be a product of Ching-te-chen in Chianghsi Province, the "ceramic capital" of China.

Published: Bibl. 23, p. 399, fig. 526; Bibl. 26, cat. no. 119 (ill.); Bibl. 41, p. 97, ill. 260; *CMAB* (January 1963), pp. 3-4, fig. 3.

62. Wine Jar

Yüan dynasty
Tz'u-chou ware, stoneware; H. 12 1/2 in. (31.8 cm.)
Worcester R. Warner Collection 17.299

Four loop handles are placed just below the mouth. A white slip and thin transparent glaze cover the inside of the neck and the outside of the jar, finishing in an uneven line just above the flaring foot. There are sections, notably under the handles, where the natural body, revealed beneath the transparent glaze, seems to have a salmon coloring. The four characters placed between the handles read: "Enough to spare year after year."

This jar has been classified as "Tc 31," a type from the late Chin-early Yüan dynasties, the probable provenance of which is Yü-hsien, Honan Province, or perhaps Shenhsi (Bibl. 46).

Published: Bibl. 26, cat. no. 44 (ill.); Bibl. 46, p. 112.

63. Jar

Yüan dynasty
Tz'u-chou ware, buff-gray stoneware; H. 11 in. (27.9 cm.)
Purchase, J. H. Wade Fund 48.215

The black-brown designs are painted into a transparent glaze, applied over a white slip which covers all but the deeply recessed base. Four daisies, separated by leaves, form a band on the shoulder. Within the areas that separate the main designs—a dragon and a highly stylized phoenix

with wings spread—are flower and cloud (or wave) patterns.

A very similar jar was excavated from beneath a wall of the thirteenth-century Yüan capital (Ta-tu) in Pei-ching, Hopei Province, in 1972. See Tokyo National Museum, *Chūka jimmin kyōwakoku shutsudō benbutsu ten* [Archaeological Treasures Excavated in the People's Republic of China; June 9-July 20, 1973], pls. 228, 231; and Special Issue of *Asahi-graph*, June 20, 1973, ill. p. 141.

Published: Bibl. 23, p. 398, fig. 524; Bibl. 26, cat. no. 45 (ill.); Bibl. 31, ill. p. 214; *CMAB* (October 1949), pp. 159-60, ill. p. 163.

64. Potter with Double-gourd Vase

Yüan dynasty
Ch'ing-pai ware, porcelain; H. 5 1/8 in. (13.1 cm.)
Severance and Greta Millikin Purchase Fund 73.14

A bluish-gray glaze covers all but the underside; a black-brown glaze highlights the hat and parts of the garment. At the back, the glaze terminates unevenly above the base, and there is a hole between the figure's shoulders. The double-gourd, or calabash, can be used as a canteen to carry water or to hold medicinal powders. Quite early in history it acquired various Taoist associations (see No. 19).

65. Chüeh

Ming dynasty, Yung-lo reign (1403-1424)
White porcelain; H. 6 in. (15.3 cm.)
John L. Severance Fund 57.59

The prototype of this libation chalice is the ancient bronze ritual vessel known as *chüeh*, dating from the Shang dynasty (ca. 1550-ca. 1025 B.C.). A bluish white glaze covers all but the flat bases of the three tall, triangular legs. There is a spur between each of the legs. Several small brown dots, glaze imperfections, are found inside the bowl at the bottom.

66. Mei-p'ing Vase

Ming dynasty, Yung-lo reign (1403-1424)
White porcelain; H. 12 5/8 in. (32.1 cm.)
Greta and Severance A. Millikin Collection 64.167

The incised, underglaze decoration is composed of floral clusters within cloud scrolls on the shoulder; lotus plants in the central area; and, near the base, below a double, incised line, a pattern of leaf scrolls. A transparent glaze covers the white porcelain except for the slightly concave base.

Published: Bibl. 23, p. 419, fig. 552.

Appendix: Seals and Colophons

1. Seals: Seal of Northern Sung government; seal of Ming government; seal of Liang Ch'ing-piao (1620-1691); seal of An I-chou (1683-ca. 1742); seal of Emperor Ch'ien-lung (r. 1736-1795); seal of Keng Chao-chung (1640-1686).

2. Seals and colophons: The top left seal has the cyclical date *ping-ch'en* (1256); the lower left seal is the Seal for Imperial Calligraphy; seal of Chu Sheng-chai (20th c.) remounted onto the facing leaf.

The inscription between the two imperial seals on the left reads, "Presented to Chung-kuei." In the colophon on a sheet attached to this leaf, Chang Ta-ch'ien (20th c.) states incorrectly that the calligraphy was personally written by the Emperor Kao-tsung (r. 1127-1162). It was suggested by Chu Sheng-chai that the recipient of this calligraphy, Chung-kuei, was a painter, Wang Chung-kuei, for whom Emperor Kao-tsung once wrote an inscription. However, this attribution is untenable because of the now determined date of the fan as recorded by Wang K'o-yü in his *San-hu-wang (Netted Corals)*. (See catalogue entry No. 3 for an explanation of the correct dating of this leaf.) During the reign of Li-tsung there was an accomplished scholar, Yeh Ts'ai, who held a high position in the government, being the "Mi-shu-chien," and whose *tzu* was Chung-kuei; however, it is not common for an emperor to refer to a subject by his *tzu*.

4. Seals: Seal of Ashikaga Yoshimitsu (r. 1368-1394), third shōgun of the Muromachi period (1338-1573); 2 seals too faint to discern.

5. Seals: Seal of Ashikaga Yoshimitsu (r. 1368-1394), third shōgun of the Muromachi period (1338-1573); 2 seals too faint to discern.

6. Seals: Poem and seal of Ch'ih-chüeh Tao-ch'ung (first half of 13th c.). Ch'ih-chüeh lived at the T'ien-t'ung Monastery, west of T'ien-t'ung mountain, within the famous T'ai-po mountain of the Ssu-ming range (Yin-hsien, Chechiang Province). The monastery's name was changed to Hung-fa in the mid-1600's. During the reign of Emperor Li-tsung (1225-1264), the mayor of Hang-chou asked him to bring Ch'ih-chüeh Tao-ch'ung to Hang-chou to be head of a newly constructed temple. The Emperor so ordered.

7. Seals: Seal at lower left, which reads, "Mountain dweller of the cloudy islet" (*Yün-chou shan-jen*).

8. Seals and colophons: Colophon above the painting on the mounting, dated summer of *yi-ch'ou* (1625); 2 seals of Kao P'an-lung (1562-1626); 2 seals on lower left mounting of Liu Shu (1759-1816); seal of Pi Lung (late 18th c.) at the bottom right corner below 2 seals too faint to discern; title mounted at top right and 3 seals of a Mr. T'ang of Pi-ling, Chiangsu Province; seal above the painting at the left of Ts'ao Tzu-wen.

9. Seal: The seal, "Tz'u-p'ing," is presumably that of Yen Tz'u-p'ing, a mid-12th-c. painter; it is, however, a later interpolation, probably Japanese. The attribution to this artist by Kanō Tsunenobu (1636-1713) cannot be sustained.

10. Seals and colophons: Colophon and 2 seals of Han Hsing (1266-1341); colophon of Ch'iu Yüan (b. 1261); colophon of Cheng Yüan-yu (1292-1364); colophon of Wu K'e-kung (d. after 1341); colophon and 2 seals of Ang Chi (act. mid-14th c.); colophon and seal of Wang Tzu-fang; colophon and 2 seals of K'o Chiu-ssu (1290-1343); colophon and seal of Yü Li (act. mid-14th c.); colophon dated 1351 and seal of Chao I (son of Chao Meng-fu); colophon and seal of Yü Chi (1272-1348); colophon and 2 seals of Sun Shih (act. early 15th c.); colophon and seal of Chang Chu (1287-1368); colophon and 2 seals of Chang Wu (act. 1335-1365); colophon dated 1348 and seal of Ch'en Chi (1314-1370); colophon of Chang Shen (act. 2nd half of 14th c.); colophon and 3 seals of Wang Hsün; colophon and 2 seals of Hu Kuang-ta; colophon and 3 seals of Wang Yin-shih; colophon and 4 seals of Chang Yü-ch'u (d. 1410);

colophon and seal of Yao Kuang-hsiao (1335-1419); colophon and 3 seals of Wang Ning (late 14-early 15th c.); colophon and 5 seals of Ou-yang An (act. early 15th c.); colophon and 3 seals of Ch'en Lien (ca. 1368-1398); colophon dated 1434 and 5 seals of Wei Chi (1374-1471); colophon and 3 seals of Chang I (act. ca. 1465-1487); colophon and 5 seals of Yin Chih (ca. 1454); colophon of Tsou Yü; seal of Ch'eng Cheng-k'uei (act. 1631-1674); 16 seals of Liang Ch'ing-piao (1620-1691); colophon dated 1629 and 2 seals of Hsü Shou-ho (act. ca. 1st half of 17th c.); colophon and 2 seals of Hsü Shu-tung (who remounted the painting in 1802); 2 seals of Wu T'ing (18th c.); 3 seals of T'ang Tso-mei (late 18th-early 19th c.).

11. Seals and colophons: Colophon and seal at top right by Shen Meng-lin (mid-14th c.); seal at top center of Prince I (18th c.).

12. Seals and colophons: Poem and seal of Shen Chou (1427-1509); 7 seals of Liang Ching-piao (1620-1691); seal of Wang I-jung (1848-1900); seal of Li Chao-heng (act. 1st half of 17th c.); 2 colophons and 8 seals of Ch'en Jen-t'ao (20th c.); seal of Li Yen-shan (20th c.).

13. Seals: 8 seals of Keng Chao-chung (1640-1686); 2 seals of Keng Chia-tso (son of Chao-chung).

A spurious signature of Wang Meng (ca. 1309-1385) that was once at the top right corner over Sheng Mou's signature was removed from the album leaf before it came into the museum's collection.

14. Seals and colophons: 2 seals of Yang Shih-ch'i (1365-1444); 2 seals of An Kuo (1481-1534); 8 seals of Hsiang Yüan-pien (1525-1590); 4 seals of Keng Chao-chung (1640-1686); 4 seals and the title, "Ch'iu-yüeh mo-huan" (Ch'iu-yüeh's Ink Fantasy), written by Niu Shu-yü (1760-1827); 4 seals of P'u T'ung (20th c.); 6 seals of T'an Ching (20th c.); seal of Liu Ting-chih (20th c.).

The artist's signature is somewhat obscured by damage, but the painting is apparently identical with the picture cited in *Shih-ku-t'ang shu-hua hui-k'ao* by Pien Yung-yü (1644-1712), written in 1680-1682, where mention is made of two colophons, now missing; one dated 1389, by Yü Ho, and one by Wu K'uan (1435-1504). The Cleveland scroll fits perfectly the description detailed in Yü Ho's colophon. According to the catalogue of the Yeh Kung-cho collection, published in 1964 (*Hsia-an ch'ing-pi-en*), these colophons were removed to another handscroll of the same subject (on paper) which was in the Yeh Kung-cho collection at that time. (For details see Bibl. 26, no. 206.) A translation of the first and last parts of the colophon by Yü Ho have been published (Bibl. 26); the remaining section, which should follow the first part, reads:

By request of [Sha] Yen-te, I venture this inscription: I heard that the legendary Chung K'uei was a native of Chung-nan (Shenhsi Province), who killed himself under the stone steps because of his failure in the civil service examination. He was consequently bestowed the official robe and sceptre of a chin-shih. Then in a dream of the Emperor Hsüan-tsung he manifested himself, saying: "Your servant should destroy all the 'squandering evils' of the world for Your Majesty." Is it possible that this painting has something to do with that dream? However, demons have no form and cannot be seen. How could they possess such forms as in the painting? Could this be only a tour-de-force of the painter who exhausted the possibilities of something nonexistent? But even nonexistence could sometimes be illustrative: Even after his death, the chin-shih *of Chung-nan could still be able to destroy evils for the world. Should a living man not alert himself after seeing this painting? Indeed, the moral is profound in the subtleties of a great master's ideas.* [trans. Wai-kam Ho]

The colophon by Wu K'uan reads:

Yen Ch'iu-yüeh, named Hui, was a native of Chiang-shan in the Yüan period.

He was born gifted, having the cultured demeanor of a scholar. He was good in figure painting and Taoist and Buddhist subjects. He was said to have died and then revived, and consequently was especially good in ghost painting. This handscroll depicts Chung K'uei's excursion in the New Year's night. The brushwork is so extraordinary that it shows an "eight-sided liveliness" (i.e., liveliness from all sides). It awes anyone who unrolls the scroll. No one could achieve such wonder unless he had penetrated the secrets of the creator. May it be treasured as a precious jade and handed down from generation to generation. [signed] Wu K'uan of Yen-ling. [trans. Wai-kam Ho]

15. Seals and colophons: Colophon dated 1360 and 23 seals of Ch'u Huan; colophon dated 1785 and 3 seals of Lu Shih-hua (1714-1779); colophon dated 1935 of Yeh Kung-cho; colophon dated 1935 of Wu Hu-fan; colophon dated 1938 and seal of Wang T'ing-yü (1855-ca. 1940); colophon dated 1941 of Wu Hua-yüan; colophon dated 1942 and 7 seals of Hsü Pang-ta; colophon dated 1942 of Lang Ching-shan; colophon dated 1944 of T'ang Yün; 5 seals of Wang Chi-ch'ien (20th c.).

The inscription by the calligrapher Ch'u Huan reads:

In the foregoing is The Nine Songs *from Li-sao based on the original of Lung-mien chü-shih [Li Kung-lin, 1049-1106] and painted by Chang Wu, t. Shu-hou, of Huai-nan. The painting is a wonder unsurpassed in our time. It has been in the family collection of . . . who has asked me to write the text. I therefore recorded this as above. Noted by Ch'u Huan of Honan on the first day of the third month of the year hsin-ch'ou, the twenty-first year of the reign Chih-cheng [1360].* [Bibl. 26]

The colophon by Lu Shih-hua (1714-1779) is translated in Bibl. 26 and thus omitted here.

This painting is probably the last one of three versions of *The Nine Songs* reliably ascribed in Chinese literature to Chang Wu: (1) with an inscription by Pei Ch'iung, dated 1376; (2) with the text written by Wu Meng-tzu, dated 1346; (3) with the text written by Ch'u Huan, dated 1360, and an inscription by Ni Tsan, dated 1372. (For detailed sources on the history of these versions, see Bibl. 26.)

17. Seals and colophons: Title page written by Chang Pi (Yüan dynasty); colophon dated 1360 and 2 seals of Yang Wei-cheng (1296-1370); colophon and 3 seals of Wang I; colophon of Chang Chün-te; colophon and 3 seals of Ang Chi (act. ca. mid-14th c.); colophon and seal of Hsü Shih-ch'üan; colophon and 3 seals of Kao Yü; colophon and 2 seals of Li Ming-fu; colophon and 2 seals of Lü Lin; colophon and seal of Chang Ch'ien; colophon of T'ao T'ang-wen; colophon and seal of Wu Yüan-kuei (act. ca. 1300-1360); colophon of Pao Chiung; colophon of Wang Tsao; colophon and seal of Ma Ch'u-i; colophon and seal of Lin I-chuang; colophon and seal of Ku Shun-chü; colophon and 2 seals of Wang Ching; colophon and 2 seals of Lin Shou-ch'ang; colophon and seal of Kao Chih-tao; colophon of Lin Hsün; colophon dated 1359 and 2 seals of Meng Wei-ch'eng (act. mid-14th c.); colophon and seal of Meng Chih-ch'i (act. mid-14th c.); 14 seals of Liang Ch'ing-piao (1620-1691); poem dated 1755 and 5 seals of Emperor Ch'ien-lung (1711-1799); 2 seals of Emperor Chia-ch'ing (1736-1795); 3 seals of the last emperor, Hsüan-t'ung (r. 1909-1912).

The title of this painting, and of Yang Wei-ching's colophon, "An Essay on Leisure to Spare," is surely an allusion to the poetry of T'ao Yüan-ming (or T'ao Ch'ien, ca. 370-427), perhaps the most famous poet-hermit in China's history. In the year 405 he left the "dusty net" of the official world at P'eng-tse and returned to his home, a thatched cottage near the present-day Chiu-ch'iang, Chianghsi Province. It was probably during that year that he wrote his famous *Kuei-ch'ü-lai (Home Again)* and *Kuei-t'ien-yüan-chü (Return to Dwell in the Country).* It is in the first verse of the latter set of poems that the phrase *yu-yü-hsien* (leisure enough to spare) is used, in the last line of the penultimate couplet.

18. Seals and colophons: At the upper right are a seal and a poem of Ch'u-shih Fan-ch'i (1297-1371).

Presumably this painting and four others by Yin-t'o-lo, registered as National Treasures in Japan, are part of an original handscroll depicting subjects concerned with Ch'an enlightenment. The scroll was cut into separate segments after its importation to Japan.

Yin-t'o-lo was a monk at the temple of Ta-kuang-chiao in K'ai-feng. There is evidence, though dubious, that he was a priest at the temple of Chung-t'ien-chu while Ch'u-shih Fan-ch'i had secluded himself there (see *Kundaikan Sochoki,* the 15th-century catalogue by Noami and Soami).

19. Seals and colophons: 4 seals of Wang Shih-min (1592-1680); 2 seals of Kung Hsiang-lin (1658-1733); colophon at the left, dated 1684, of Yen Sheng-sun (1623-1702); colophon at the right and seal of Huang Jen (1683-1768);

seal of Lu Hsin-yüan (1834-1894); 2 seals of Lu Shu-shen (3rd son of Lu Hsin-yüan); 3 seals of T'ao Kuang; seal of T'an Ching (20th c.); 4 seals of Chang Heng (1915-1963).

20. The particular kind of sized paper used here, *feng-chien,* or powdered paper, was by no means rare during the late 14th century. Liu Chi, a scholar of the time, remarked, "Calligraphy written on *feng-chien* cannot last long; this is especially true in recent years as the products become rather crude and not refined enough. Writings on this kind of paper will begin to flake off in less than one or two years." (From *Fei-hsüeh lu* [Notes in Driven Snow], Ku-chin shuo-hai edition, ch. 2, p. 3a.)

This seems to be the best explanation for the present condition of the Cleveland scroll. Not only have the painter's inscriptions been seriously affected by the flaking of the powdered surface, but the painting, too, has suffered considerably in its loss of the original richness of ink tones and the subtlety of the brush strokes. It remains, however, a very rare example of ink-flower painting in the *pai-miao* style of the 14th century, and is possibly the only published surviving work of the artist Chao Chung.

21. Seals: 9 seals of collectors, Wang Chi-ch'ien (20th c.), Chang Ta-ch'ien (20th c.), and others.

This painting is the only known work by Liu Shan-shou, an artist not yet discovered in the historical sources.

22. Seals: Seal of Tuan Fang (1861-1911); unidentified seal.

Since Lo Chih-ch'uan was published by Shimada (*Ho-un,* no. 22, Kyoto, 1938), only this and one other painting have been identified by Wai-kam Ho as being by his brush. (For the other painting see Richard Barnhart, *Wintry Forests, Old Trees,* exhibition catalogue, China Institute, New York, 1972.)

24. Seals and colophons: Poem and 2 seals of the priest Liao-an Ch'ing-yü (Seijoku).

28. Seals: 6 seals of Emperor Ch'ien-lung (r. 1735-1796); seal of Emperor Chia-ch'ing (r. 1796-1820); 2 half seals of the Ch'ien family.

Seals often supply information beyond that of merely who owned the painting, and the imperial seals on the present painting are one such example. During the Ch'ing dynasty there were three editions (compilations ending in 1745, 1793, and 1817) of a catalogue of the imperial collection of calligraphy and painting entitled *Shih-chü pao-chi.* The seals at the right edge, and the round seal at the far left at the upper edge, of the painting are those of Emperor Ch'ien-lung (Kao-tsung). They not only reveal that this painting is recorded in the first edition of the imperial catalogue, but also indicate that the compilers considered this painting to be among the top grade of paintings in the collection. Paintings so classified have detailed entries in the first edition which record size, medium, inscriptions, seals, and colophons. This information is very helpful in the reconstruction of the history of the painting.

The ordering of the catalogue is by palaces and halls. The lowest seal at the right edge of *Old Pine Tree,* which designates the name of the palace or hall in which the painting was located, thus aids in locating the catalogue entry. The first oval seal at the right above the branch proves that the painting was in the imperial collection during the reign of Emperor Chia-ch'ing (Jen-tsung). The painting by Yao T'ing-mei (No. 17) carries five imperial seals, indicating that it also was considered top grade by the compilers of the first edition, and giving its location. The painting by Tung Ch'i-ch'ang (No. 32) bears seals revealing that it was recorded in the second edition. For a fairly complete explanation of the imperial seals and catalogues, see Na Chih-liang, *Hsi-yin t'ung-shih* (Taipei, 1970).

29. Seals and colophons: Title page dated 1786 and 2 seals of Wang Wen-chih (1730-1802); colophon and 2 seals of Ni Yüeh (1444-1501).

31. Seals: 4 seals of Chu Ching-hou.

32. Seals and colophons: 2 colophons and 8 seals of Kao Shih-ch'i (1645-1704); colophon and 2 seals of Sung Lo (1634-1713); 2 colophons and 11 seals of Emperor Ch'ien-lung (r. 1735-1796); colophon and 2 seals of Shao Ch'ang-heng; seal of Wang Chi-ch'ien (20th c.). See No. 28 above for information on the imperial seals.

33. Seal: Collector's seal at the bottom right.

34. Seals: 2 seals of Ch'eng Ch'i (20th c.).

35. Seals: 4 seals of T'ang Tso-mei (late 18th-early 19th c.); 7 seals of Chang Heng (1915-1963); and one not yet identified.

36. Seals and colophons: Colophon dated 1699 and 5 seals of Kao Shih-ch'i (1645-1704).

Bibliography

In the colophon, Kao describes the scenery and explains that the mountains of the five cataracts are at the borders of Wu-chou, Hang-chou, and Yüeh-chou (Shao-hsing), and are close to Chi-yang (or Chu-chi, Ch'en Hung-shou's home) in Chechiang Province. Among other things, this connoisseur of the K'ang-hsi period stated that Ch'en Hung-shou imitated the mountains and rocks of the artists of the Six Dynasties period and the trees of Tung Yüan (act. ca. 945), and in general captured the interplay of light, shade, and distances created by the seventy-two peaks.

37. Seal: One collector's seal.

41. Colophons: A leaf of inscriptions accompanies the painting, with colophons by Ma Yüeh-kuan (1688–1755) and Huang Ts'ou, a pupil of the famous artist Fang Shih-shu (1692–1751).

45. Seals and colophons: 2 seals of Chang Ta-ch'ien (20th c.) on mounting at right; colophon and seal of a modern Chinese collector. The colophon reads:

> *Heaven forsook the imperial house of the Ming dynasty and gave birth to a great master of painting. The idea of Chuang Chou about the happiness of the fish does not necessarily imply the life in the Pond of Jade. Lately I have not seen as many paintings by Pa-ta-shan-jen as before the political turmoil. Now, during my withdrawal at home, I was so fortunate to be able to handle this scroll and enjoy it under the window on a fine day. I feel that water and ink are so rich that they create a particularly inspiring flavor. Indeed the painting should not be evaluated merely from its surface. Respectfully, I did this colophon for the master of the Hermitage of Grapes. [signed] Ta-han-chü-shih.* [trans. Wai-kam Ho]

The philosopher Chuang Chou, also known as Chuang-tzu (b. ca. 370 B.C.), had a famous argument with Hui-tzu, held on a bridge, about how it was possible that he, Chuang-tzu, could know the happiness of the fish swimming about beneath them.

46. Seal: Seal of P'ang Yüan-chi (20th c.).

47. Seals: Seal of Wang Chi-ch'ien (20th c.); others.

The following is a list of publications mentioned more than once in the catalogue. It is not intended to serve as a selected bibliography for reading, although many of the publications might well be included in such a list.

1. *Archives of the Chinese Art Society of America* (vols. I-XIX, 1945–65). *Archives of Asian Art* (begins with vol. XX, 1966–67).

2. Cahill, James. *The Art of Southern Sung China.* Catalogue of an exhibition at Asia House Gallery, New York, 1962.

3. Cahill, James. *Fantastics and Eccentrics in Chinese Painting.* Catalogue of an exhibition at Asia House Gallery, New York, 1967.

4. Chang Wan-li and Hu Jen-mou. *The Selected Painting and Calligraphy of Pa-ta-shan-jen*, vol. I. Hong Kong, 1969.

5. Cheng Chen-to. *Yün-hui-chai ts'ang T'ang, Sung i-lai ming-hua-chi* [Paintings of the T'ang, Sung, and Later Periods in the Collection of Chang Ts'ung-yü]. Shanghai, 1947.

6. Christie, Anthony. *Chinese Mythology.* London, 1968.

7. Contag, Victoria. *Chinese Masters of the 17th Century.* Rutland, Vt., 1970.

8. Cox, Warren. *The Book of Pottery and Porcelain.* 2 vols. New York, 1944.

9. Dubosc, Jean Pierre. *Mostra d'arte Cinese.* Catalogue of an exhibition at the Palazzo Ducale, Venice, 1954.

10. Ferguson, John. *Li-tai chu-lu hua-mu* [Index of Recorded Chinese Paintings in All Periods]. Nanking, 1933.

11. Goepper, Roger. *Chinesische Malerei die alter Tradition.* Bern, 1960.

12. Goepper, Roger. *The Essence of Chinese Painting.* London, 1963.

13. Harada, Kinjiro. *Shina meiga hōkan* [Pageant of Chinese Painting]. Tokyo, 1936.

14. Hasabe, Rakuji, ed. "Wares Made by Several Kilns in North China of the Sung Dynasty," *Toki Zenshu*, vol. 13, Tokyo, 1958.

15. Hasabe, Rakuji. "Chinese Ceramics of the Tenth Century," *Proceedings of the Tokyo National Museum*, vol. III. Tokyo, 1967.

16. *Horizon Book of the Arts of China.* New York, 1969.

17. Hsieh Chih-liu. *T'ang, Wu-tai, Sung, Yüan ming-chi* [Paintings of the T'ang, Five Dynasties, Sung, and Yüan Dynasties]. Shanghai, 1957.

18. Koyama, Fujio. "Hsiu Wu Ceramic Kilns in the Northern Sung Dynasty, China," *Bijutsu Kenkyu*, vol. VI, no. CLXI (1950).

19. Lee, Sherman. *Chinese Landscape Painting.* Catalogue of an exhibition at The Cleveland Museum of Art, Cleveland, 1954.

20. Lee, Sherman. "Some Problems in Ming and Ch'ing Landscape Painting," *Ars Orientalis*, vol. 2 (1957), pp. 471–85.

21. Lee, Sherman. "Contrasts in Chinese and Japanese Art," *Journal of Aesthetics and Art Criticism*, vol. XXI (Fall 1962), pp. 3–12.

22. Lee, Sherman. *Chinese Landscape Painting.* New York, 1962.

23. Lee, Sherman. *A History of Far Eastern Art.* New York, 1964.

24. Lee, Sherman. "Scattered Pearls Beyond the Ocean," *Cleveland Museum of Art Bulletin*, vol. LI (February 1964), pp. 22–39.

25. Lee, Sherman. "Literati and Professionals: Four Ming Painters," *Cleveland Museum of Art Bulletin*, vol. LIII (January 1966), pp. 3–25.

26. Lee, Sherman, and Wai-kam Ho. *Chinese Art Under the Mongols: The Yüan Dynasty.* Catalogue of an exhibition at The Cleveland Museum of Art, Cleveland, 1968.

27. Lee, Sherman. "The Water and the Moon in Chinese and Modern Painting," *Art International*, vol. XIV, no. 1 (January 1970), pp. 47–59.

28. Lee, Sherman. "To See Big within Small: Hsiao-Chung-Chien-Ta," *The Burlington Magazine*, vol. CXIV, no. 830 (May 1972), pp. 314–22.

29. Lovell, Hin-cheung. *Illustrated Catalogue of Ting Yao and Related White Wares in the Percival David Foundation of Chinese Art.* London, 1964.

30. Munich. Haus der Kunst. *1000 Jahre Chinesische Malerei.* Catalogue of an exhibition at the Haus der Kunst, Munich, 1959.

31. Plumer, James. "The Potter's Art at Cleveland," *American Magazine of Art*, April 1940, pp. 212–17.

32. *Praeger Encyclopedia of Art.* 5 vols. New York, 1971.

33. Sirén, Osvald. *Chinese Painting: Leading Masters and Principles.* 7 vols. London, 1956–58.

34. Smith College Museum of Art, Northampton, Mass. *Chinese Art: An Exhibition of Paintings, Jades, Bronzes and Ceramics.* Catalogue of an exhibition at the Smith College Museum of Art, 1962.

35. Sullivan, Michael. *The Book of Art.* vol. IX: *Chinese and Japanese Art.* New York, 1965.

36. Sullivan, Michael. *An Introduction to Chinese Art.* London, 1961.

37. Sutton, Denys. "The New Oriental Art Galleries at Cleveland," *Apollo*, vol. XCII, no. 102 (August 1970), pp. 148–51.

38. Tokyo. Imperial Museum. *Tō-sō-genmin meiga taikan* [Catalogue of an Exhibition of Chinese Paintings of the T'ang, Sung, Yüan, and Ming Dynasties]. 2 vols. Tokyo, 1930.

39. *Chinese Art in Western Collections.* vol. V: *Ceramics.* Tokyo, 1973.

40. *Tōyō tōji ten: Chūkoku, Chōsen, Nihon* [Far Eastern Ceramics: Chinese, Korean, and Japanese]. Catalogue of an exhibition at the Tokyo National Museum, Tokyo, 1970.

41. Trubner, Henry. *Chinese Ceramics from the Prehistoric Period Through Ch'ien Lung.* Catalogue of an exhibition at the Los Angeles County Museum of Art, Los Angeles, 1952.

42. Tseng Hsien-ch'i. *Loan Exhibition of Chinese Paintings.* Catalogue of an exhibition at the Royal Ontario Museum, Toronto, 1956.

43. Wang Chi-ch'ien. *Album Leaves from the Sung and Yüan Dynasties.* Catalogue of an exhibition at China House Gallery, New York, 1970.

44. Wen Fong. "Tung Ch'i-ch'ang and the Orthodox Theory of Painting," *National Palace Museum Quarterly*, vol. II, no. 3 (1969).

45. Wen Fong. "Wang Hui, the Great Synthesis," *National Palace Museum Quarterly*, vol. III (1969).

46. Wirgin, Jan. "Sung Ceramic Designs," *The Museum of Far Eastern Antiquities Bulletin*, no. 42 (1970), pp. 1–272.

Index

The following list of names and places is derived from the material in the catalogue. The numbers after each item are catalogue numbers, and the reference may be located in the main catalogue entry, the corresponding appendix entry (for Nos. 1–47), or both.

An I-chou, 1
An Kuo, 14
An-yang, 10
Ang Chi, 10, 17
Ashikaga Yoshimitsu, 4, 5

Bodhidharma, 9, 24
Buddha, *see* Shakyamuni

Ch'a Shih-piao, 41, 42
Chang Ch'ien, 17
Chang Chu, 10
Chang Chün-te, 17
Chang Heng, 19, 35
Chang I, 10
Ch'ang-pai, Mt., 42
Chang Pi, 17
Chang Seng-yu, 10
Chang Shen, 10
Ch'ang-shu, 46
Chang Ta-ch'ien, 2, 21, 45
Chang Wu, 10, 15
Chang Yü-ch'u, 10
Chao Chung, 20
Chao Hsiang, 29
Chao I, 10
Chao Kuei-ch'eng, *see* Li-tsung
Chao Meng-fu, 10, 25
Chao Yün, *see* Li-tsung
Ch'en Chi, 10
Ch'en Ch'i, 34
Ch'en Hung-shou, 36
Ch'en Jen-t'ao, 12
Ch'en Ju-yen, 19
Ch'en Lien, 10
Ch'eng Cheng-k'uei, 10
Cheng Yüan-yu, 10
Chi-ch'iu, 11
Chia-ch'ing, Emperor, 17, 28

Chia-hsing, 12, 13, 35
Chia-ting, 33
Chiang-shan, 14
Chiang Shen, 8
Chiao Fang, 29
Chiao-tso, 51
Ch'ien family, 28
Ch'ien-lung, 1, 17, 28, 32
Ch'ien-t'ang, 4, 5, 34
Chien-tz'u Ts'un, 58
Ch'ih-chüeh Tao-chung, 6
Chih-tun, 34
Ching Hao, 44, 47
Ching-te-chen, 61
Ch'iu-chiang, 17
Ch'iu Yüan, 10
Chou Hao, 30
Chu-chi, 36
Chu Ching-hou, 31
Ch'u Huan, 15
Chü-jan, 1, 12, 40
Chu Sheng-chai, 2
Ch'u-shih Fan-ch'i, 18
Ch'u state, 15
Chu Ta, 45
Chu Tao-sheng, 27
Ch'ü-yang, 58
Ch'ü Yüan, 15
Chuang Chou, or Chuang-tzu, 45
Chung K'uei, 14
Chung-kuei, 2
Chung-nan mountain, 2, 14
Chung-t'ien-chu temple, 18

Daruma, *see* Bodhidharma
Diamond Sutra, 27

Fa-ch'ang, *see* Mu Ch'i
Fang Shih-shu, 41
Fen-chou, 52
Feng Chüeh, 29
Fu Han, 29

Han Hsing, 10
Hang-chou, 2, 3, 6, 15
Ho Lung, 26
Honan Temmoku, 55
Hsi-hsien, 33

Hsiang Sheng-mo, 35
Hsiang Yüan-pien, 14
Hsiang Yung, 47
Hsiao Yün-ts'ung, 38
Hsiu-ning, 41, 42
Hsiu-wu, 51
Hsü Hao, 14
Hsü Pang-ta, 15
Hsü Shih-ch'üan, 17
Hsü Shou-ho, 10
Hsü Shu-tung, 10
Hsüan-ch'eng, 43, 44
Hsüan-tsung (of T'ang), 14
Hsüan-t'ung, 17
Hu Kuang-ta, 10
Hua-ting, *see* Sung-chiang
Huang, Mr., 45
Huang Jen, 19
Huang Kung-wang, 32, 33, 42
Huang Ts'ou, 41
Hui-k'o, 9
Hui-tsung, 1, 14
Hui-tzu, 45
Hung-fa monastery, 6
Hung-jen, 18

I, Prince, 11
I Weng, 46

K'ai-feng, 1, 18
Kano Tsunenobu, 9
Kao Chih-tao, 17
Kao Ko-kung, 37
Kao P'an-lung, 8
Kao Shih-ch'i, 32, 36
Kao-tsu, 14
Kao-tsung (of Sung), 2, 46
Kao-tsung (of Ch'ing), *see* Ch'ien-lung
Kao Yü, 17
Keng Chao-chung, 1, 13, 14
Keng Chia-tso, 13
K'o Chiu-ssu, 10
Ko Hung, 19
Ku Shun-chü, 17
Ku Te-hui, 10
Ku Ying, 10
Kuan T'ung, 44, 47

Kuang-chou, 9, 19
Kumārajīva, 27
K'un-shan, 39, 40
Kung Hsiang-lin, 19
Kung Hsien, 37, 39, 40
Kuo Hsi, 23, 46

Lan Ying, 34
Lang Ching-shan, 15
Li Chao-heng, 12
Li Ch'eng, 23
Li Ho, 20
Li Kung-lin, 15
Li Liu-fang, 33
Li Ming-fu, 17
Li Shih-cho, 47
Li Shih-hsing, 11
Li-tsung, 2, 3, 6
Li Tung-yang, 29
Li Yen-shan, 12
Liang Ch'ing-piao, 1, 10, 12, 17
Liao-an Ching-yü, 24
Lin-chiang, 22
Lin Hsün, 17
Lin I-chuang, 17
Lin Shou-ch'ang, 17
Liu Chi, 20
Liu Shan-shou, 21
Liu Shu, 8
Liu Ting-chih, 14
Liu-t'ung monastery, 4, 5
Liu-yün-ho, 37
Lo Chih-ch'uan, 22
Lo-fou mountain, 19
Lo-yang, 9
Lü Ch'ang, 29
Lu Chih, 31
Lu Hsin-yüan, 19
Lu Lin, 17
Lu Shih-hua, 15
Lu Shu-shen, 19
Lu Yü, 26
Lung-hsi, 25

Ma Ch'u-i, 17
Ma Lin, 2, 3
Ma Yüeh-kuan, 41
Mei Ch'ing, 43, 44

Meng Chih-ch'i, 17
Meng Wei-ch'eng, 17
Mi Fei, 41
Mi-lo River, 15
Ming Huang, *see* Hsüan-tsung
Mu Ch'i, 4, 5

Nan-ch'ang, 45
Nan-ching, 1, 37
Ni Tsan, 15, 31, 33
Ni Yüeh, 29
Nirvāna Sutra, 27
Niu Shu-yü, 14

Ou-yang An, 10

P'ang Yüan-chi, 46
Pao Chiung, 17
Pao-ying, 29
Pei-ching (Peking), 10, 25, 63
Pei Ch'iung, 15
P'eng Hsü, 30
P'eng-tse, 17
Pi Lung, 8
Pien-liang, *see* K'ai-feng
Pien Wen-chin, 25, 52
Pien Yung-yü, 14
P'u Ming, 16
P'u T'ung, 14

San-han, 47
Seijoku, 24
Sha-hsien, 25
Sha Yen-te, 14
Shakyamuni, 6
Shan-fu, 10
Shao Ch'ang-heng, 32
Shao-lin temple, 9, 24
Shao Sung-nien, 1
Shen Chou, 12, 26, 27, 43
Shen Meng-lin, 11
Shen-tsung, *see* Wan-li
Sheng Mao-yeh, 37
Sheng Mou, 13
Shih-chü pao-chi, 28
Ssu-ch'i, 19
Ssu-ming mountains, 6
Su-chou, 19, 26, 27, 28, 31
Sun Shih, 10

Sung-chiang, 16, 32
Sung Lo, 32
Sung, Mt., 9

Ta-kuang-chiao temple, 18
Ta-tu, 63
T'ai-po mountain, 6
T'an Ching, 14, 19
T'ang Cheng-chung, 20
T'ang Tso-mei, 10, 35
Tang-yang-yü, 51
T'ang Yün, 15
T'ao Ch'eng, 29
T'ao Ch'ien, *see* T'ao Yüan-ming
T'ao Hung, 37
T'ao Kuang, 19
Tao-sheng, *see* Chu Tao-sheng
T'ao T'ang-wen, 17
T'ao Yüan-ming, 17
Tea Classic, 26
Teng-feng, 24, 50, 51
T'ien-shui, 25
T'ien-t'ung monastery, 6
Ts'ao Tzu-wen, 8
Tsou Yü, 10
Tuan Fang, 22
Tung Ch'i-ch'ang, 28, 32
Tung Yüan, 36, 40, 41
Tzu-ch'i, 31
Tzu-wen, Professor, 46

Wan I, 17
Wan-li, 32
Wang Chi-ch'ien, 15, 21, 32, 47
Wang Ching, 17
Wang-ch'uan, 2
Wang Chung-kuei, 2
Wang Hsi-chih, 10
Wang Hsien-chih, 10
Wang Hsün, 10
Wang Hui, 46
Wang I-jung, 12
Wang K'o-yü, 2
Wang Meng, 13, 46
Wang Mien, 30
Wang Ning, 10
Wang Shih-min, 19
Wang T'ing-yü, 15

Wang Tsao, 17
Wang Tzu-fang, 10
Wang Wei, 2, 3
Wang Wen-chih, 29
Wang Yin-shih, 10
Wei Chi, 10
Wen Cheng-ming, 28, 31
Wen T'ung, 46
West Lake, 4, 5
Wu Chen, 12, 38
Wu-chiang, 20
Wu Chin-ming, 40
Wu Hsi-hsien, 29
Wu-hsing, 10, 17
Wu-hu, 38
Wu Hu-fan, 15
Wu Hua-yüan, 15
Wu K'e-kung, 10
Wu K'uan, 14
Wu Meng-tzu, 15
Wu Tao-tzu, 14, 47
Wu-ti, 24
Wu T'ing, 10
Wu Yüan-kuei, 17
Wu-yün, 34

Yang Pu-chih, 20, 30
Yang Shih-ch'i, 14
Yangtze River, 9, 24
Yang Wei-cheng, 17
Yao Kuang-hsiao, 10
Yao T'ing-mei, 17, 28
Yao Yüan-chih, 26
Yeh Kung-cho, 15
Yeh Ts'ai, 2
Yen Hui, 14
Yen-shan Ts'un, 58
Yen Sheng-sun, 19
Yen Tz'u-p'ing, 9
Yin Chih, 10
Yin-t'o-lo, 18
Yoshimitsu, *see* Ashikaga
    Yoshimitsu
Yü Chi, 10
Yü-ch'uan, 22
Yü Ho, 14
Yü-hsien, 62

Yü Li, 10
Yüan-tse, 12
Yün-chou shan-jen, 7

Credits

Catalogue designed by Joseph del Gaudio
Set in Alphatype Bodoni Book by York Typesetting/Peter Pica Inc., New York, N.Y.
Photographs courtesy of The Cleveland Museum of Art
The map on page 108 is based upon a map compiled by Yeh Hsien-k'ai
    and Ch'en I-jen for the Nan-hua Publishing Co. Ltd.
Printed by Eastern Press, Inc., New Haven, Conn.
Bound by Robert Burlen & Son, Inc., Bookbinders, Hingham, Mass.